NAMPEYO AND HER POTTERY

Nampeyo at Pendete Kiva. Original negative by J. R. Willis, ca. 1918.
Contemporary print by Walter Haussamen. (Walter Haussamen Collection)

NAMPEYO AND HER POTTERY

Barbara Kramer

Maps and drawings by
James Kramer

University of New Mexico Press   /   Albuquerque

#34245361

Library of Congress Cataloging-in-Publication Data
Kramer, Barbara, 1926–
Nampeyo and her pottery / Barbara Kramer;
maps and drawings by James Kramer.—1st ed.
        p.   cm.
Includes bibliographical references and index.
ISBN 0-8263-1718-9
1. Nampeyo, 1856–1942.
2. Hopi Indians—Biography.
3. Tewa Indians—Biography.
4. Hopi pottery.
I. Title.
E99.H7N354   1996
783.3′092—dc20
[B]
96–3950
CIP

Maps and drawings © 1996 by James Kramer

Contents

Part II. Her Pottery

Illustrations

In Part II

Maps

Author's Notes and Acknowledgments

Toward the end of the nineteenth century and the beginning of the twentieth, the isolated Hopi people attracted anthropologists, government representatives, missionaries, photographers and artists, and curious visitors to First Mesa on the Hopi Reservation. They wrote about the mesa residents and their "strange" customs; they collected Nampeyo's pots and they photographed her. But those times did not encourage a compassionate understanding of native people by white observers. Many of their published reports reflected attitudes alien to the culture that they observed, attitudes that could not have been countered by a people who could not read, who spoke little or no English, and who, in fact, had no written language of their own.

Nampeyo's inability to communicate in the English language explains the dearth of accurate published information concerning her life and her work. She left no diaries, letters, or records of her accomplishments or her disappointments, no commentary about her own work or that of her contemporaries. She left only unsigned vessels that are prized by collectors and displayed in museums throughout the world. They provoke an emotional response because of their visual grace; they can be touched and possessed. Black-and-white photographs of Nampeyo shaping or painting one of those vessels, however, do not evoke her passion for working with clay. The photographs are mute testimonies, images without communication.

My quest for information about Nampeyo in essays that recount lives of famous Indians and in books about pueblo pottery produced minimal, repetitive "common knowledge." Delving into original documents, first at the Laboratory of Anthropology in Santa Fe and then in archives, libraries, and special collections throughout the country, I found that most of the "facts" about the potter's life were inaccurate. The story had become a myth, unsupported by historical evidence.

After studying and photographing hundreds of Nampeyo's vessels in documented public and private collections, I found that, because no analysis of her pottery has been made, her undocumented vessels—and occasionally other Hopi vessels that have been attributed to Nampeyo—have been dated without substantiation. Erroneously, her name has become synonymous with unsigned revival Hopi pottery.

To gain more perspective on the Hopi-Tewa culture and the legacy of pottery-making, I went to the mesa of Nampeyo's home to converse with members of her family and other elders who might remember the potter and events during her life. A warm relationship with her descendants and other residents became an unexpected consequence of my research. Daisy Hooee[1] and Dewey Healing,[2] particularly, shared many hours with me recalling the days in which they had lived with their grandmother in the old stone house at the top of the trail. Other elders recounted stories about Nampeyo, while younger descendants remembered her only as an old lady living alone in the deteriorating Corn clan dwellings before her death.

Occasionally my questions were answered with prevalent "common knowledge" about the potter (see Appendix A, Published Fallacies and Erroneous Photographs). Many individual memories produced subjective interpretations of past events, but those personal stories that added significant interest to the text have been included. My purpose in this study about Nampeyo, however, was not to analyze a disparity between factions of an extended family or to exacerbate them. I have chosen, therefore, not to attribute specific quotations to one relative or another; their stories speak for themselves.

Except for my visits with Daisy at her home in Zuni, all other conversations took place in the old village of Hano on top of the mesa or in Polacca below. The year during which a conversation occurred appears after the quotation so that the reader can place it in time. It should be understood that elders speak on these pages in their second language, for they spoke Tewa as children before attending school and continued to do so all of their lives.

No chronologically coherent narrative of Nampeyo's life emerged from conversations with her descendants, but the interweaving, the comparing, and the relating of family commentary to historical records produced a portrait of a quiet, gentle potter who integrated ancient designs and shapes into a personal, contemporary style that revitalized a dying art.

Nampeyo and her Hano neighbors descended from Tewas living in New Mexico who had migrated around 1702, at the request of Hopi elders, to protect the Hopis from marauding Utes. The initial refusal by the Hopis to receive them when they arrived produced a long-standing antagonism between the two. Even now, though generally called "Hopi," her people remain "Hopi-Tewas," although to use that term throughout would be awkward. When the mesa peoples are referred to as a group, I have used the inclusive term *Hopi*. When additional definition is required, the more specific term *Tewa* is used.

During Nampeyo's childhood and youth, an order of social and religious functions governed her people's lives. Like all other residents of Hano, Nampeyo's family followed the customs of their ancestors. In describing her undocumented early years, I have not used the conditional tense but have described activities that would have occurred in the life of any Hopi-Tewa at the time.

Reports written by outside observers have spelled Hopi and Tewa words phonetically. The Hopis were called "Moquis," sometimes spelled "Mokis," and scholars still dispute the spelling of such words as *kachina*. Compiling this information, I was faced with choices. Except for quotations from printed sources, the spellings chosen are those generally accepted. In many cases, no "correct" form exists.

No history could be written without the assistance of research librarians, for they preserve the wealth of fragile old documents and records that writers study and interpret. All of the dedicated caretakers who answered letters and telephone calls, made photocopies, and searched for data have earned my deepest appreciation and respect. I am particularly grateful to Laura Holt at the Laboratory of Anthropology, Museum of New Mexico, Santa Fe, who unfailingly found the information that I required.

The study and comparison of ceramic vessels would not be possible without the assistance of the curators who catalog and preserve historic and prehistoric pottery on floor-to-ceiling shelves in storage rooms behind the locked doors and down the unmarked passageways of museums. My deepest gratitude to all who took time so that I could "feel" and photograph Nampeyo's work. Diane D. Dittemore, at the Arizona State Museum, Tucson, deserves special recognition, not only for the time she spent allowing me to photograph but also for the critical information she has provided to me over a period of time.

Unseen by the public but just as important to researchers are photo archivists. The staff of the National Anthropological Archives, National Museum of Natural History, Smithsonian Institution, was of particular help in locating photographs of Nampeyo, either by name or by obscure reference to an unnamed Hopi-Tewa potter of Hano. My appreciation extends to other photo-collection curators who provided the photographs included in this volume.

I am indebted to those working directly or indirectly in the field of Hopi studies and pueblo pottery who graciously shared information and provided insights: E. Charles Adams, Katharine Bartlett, Jonathan Batkin, Bruce Bernstein, Rick Dillingham, Frank Harlow, Byron Harvey III, Kelley Hays-Gilpin, Louis A. Hieb, Richard M. Howard, Byron Hunter, W. David Laird, Michael Stanislawski, Edwin L. Wade, and Barton Wright.

My appreciation extends to others who willingly shared relevant information in their particular fields or their experiences: Robert Ashton, William Belknap, Charlotte and Maurice Bloom, Jr., Ruth d'Arcy, Maurine Grammer, Katherine Spencer Halpern, Michael Harrison, Roland Jones,

Ernest E. Leavitt, Virginia Couse Leavitt, Luther L. Lyon, Bruce McGee, Jo Mora, Jr., Robert A. Trennert, Robert R. White, and many personal friends who searched for information useful to me or provided support. Aware of the need for a good reference book about the potter, Alexander E. Anthony, Jr., of the Adobe Gallery, Albuquerque, encouraged me, for which I am indebted.

Alph H. Sekakuku, former superintendent of the Hopi Agency, graciously took time to answer questions and make old documents available in agency headquarters in Keams Canyon, Arizona. Expressing interest in my subject, members of the staff of Jeff Bingaman, U.S. senator from New Mexico, obtained copies of federal documents for my reference. The Historical Department of the Church of Jesus Christ of Latter-day Saints and the American Baptist Historical Society shared with me or referred me to information contained in the text.

For my husband, James, I express my deepest gratitude. He shared, encouraged, and joined in the search for vessels and for information. His rapport with the old lady's spirit and with her extended family is as deep as mine.

Very personal appreciation is extended to Larry Goodwin and my daughter Joan Kramer Busick, and to my daughter Susan Kramer Erickson and her husband, David, for advice and continued encouragement.

Nampeyo's descendants have awaited publication of this book, for they themselves do not know the complete story of her life nor do they have access to the many fine examples of her work in private collections and in museums. I hope that this volume in some way expresses my heartfelt appreciation for their continued interest and their friendship.

All of the background data gathered—objective and subjective, general and specific, clearly factual and sometimes questionable—had to be analyzed and coordinated. Not all of the writings I consulted were reliable. Not all of the information collected through interviews was accurate. The sole responsibility for interpretation and presentation of the material in these pages is my own.

Part I.
Nampeyo

They say that every piece of clay
is a piece of someone's life.
            —*Byrd Baylor,* When Clay Sings

Birth

"Everything the old way." (1986)

A triangle of dissimilar geographical points in northern Arizona defines an imaginary boundary within which mingle Hopi history and the intangible world of kachina spirits. To the northwest, the gorge of the Grand Canyon meanders through a landscape of rock slowly carved over the aeons by the Colorado River. Some Hopis believe this to be the location of Sipapuni, the entrance into the present upper world from earlier worlds below.

About eighty miles to the east, the three-fingered hand of the Hopi mesas lies against mother Earth, rich in coal deposits that extend north to the Utah border, the fingers pointing southwest toward the San Francisco Peaks. Ancient villages cling to the rocky formations that are known quite simply as First, Second, and Third Mesas. Antelope Mesa, now the site of numerous pueblo ruins, spreads out like a thumb east of First Mesa, with Keams Canyon sheltered along its western base.

Eighty miles southwest from the mesas, nearly due south from the Grand Canyon, the San Francisco Peaks watch over the dry, undulating plains of this comfortless stretch of land. Their distant pyramidal silhouette casts a timeless presence upon the lives of the people. Hopis believe the peaks to be the home of supernatural kachina spirits that appear in mesa villages in the form of masked, costumed men from winter solstice to summer solstice.

Hopi legends passed down from generation to generation tell that their people had lived in three worlds below before ascending through an opening, the Sipapuni, into this the Fourth World. Upon arriving, the Hopis broke into clans to search for their rightful home. One after the other settled near the mesas, each bringing tales of adventures and special ceremonies to benefit the people. Or so the story of emergence is still told with variations to instruct the young.[1]

According to anthropological theory, the present-day Hopis are descendants of nomadic hunters who dug pit houses and later settled into an agrarian life. Groups migrating from other areas introduced the knowledge of basketry, pottery-making, and other skills. Below-ground rooms became kivas, ceremonial chambers with a symbolic Sipapuni in the center representing the navel of the Earth from which all men entered the world. Above-ground living quarters evolved into multistoried clusters of rooms.

The small villages that lay scattered throughout the region were vulnerable to attack by the Utes, Navajos, Apaches, and Comanches, so the people moved their villages to the tops of the mesas. Relocation provided defense against Spanish intrusion during the sixteenth and seventeenth centuries as well. Because nomadic bands continued to raid Hopi crops and livestock in the valleys, Hopi chiefs, according to legend, petitioned a group of Tewas known for their defiance and bravery to relocate from their pueblo in northern New Mexico to protect them.

The story of the Tewa migration is told ritually in the kivas by the old to their young so their heritage will not be forgotten.[2] The group arrived at First Mesa about 1702, but for reasons unknown to them, the Hopi chief would not fulfill the promise of land until they had proved their prowess. After a band of Utes attacked and were defeated by the Tewas, they were given a site on the mesa to build their own village. The confrontation created a divisiveness between the two people of distinctively different personalities: the conservative Hopis who adhere to tradition and the progressive Tewas who respect tradition but are willing to listen and to compromise.

The ancient villages located atop the three mesas are still

inhabited. On Third Mesa, old Oraibi has nearly crumbled back into the rock of Third Mesa, but it has been revived at the base of the mesa as New Oraibi, or Kykotsmovi, now the tribal headquarters of the Hopi Reservation. Shongopovi, Shipolovi, and Mishongnovi remain on Second Mesa, their old stone houses clustered around ancient dirt plazas. On the restrictive point of First Mesa, Walpi's jumble of dwellings are separated by a narrow path from Sichomovi, which now crowds its neighboring Tewa village to the north.

The Tewas call it Tewa Village, but it is commonly known as Hano. On the narrow top near the gap in the mesa, each Tewa clan built stone dwellings similar to those of the Hopis, and, in the traditional matriarchal society, the house belonged to the woman. When a daughter married, the husband moved to her home. As a clan increased in numbers, second- and sometimes third-story rooms would be added atop the rooms below.

Dwellings that expanded outward and upward eventually enclosed a dirt plaza where ceremonial activities and social dances took place, where members of a clan seated on sheepskins and rabbitskin blankets celebrated a marriage or the harvesting of crops with a feast. Young men courted maidens through open windows while, inside, near the grinding stones, the girls kneeled at their task of preparing cornmeal. In the northeast corner of the plaza, the Monete Kiva provided an underground chamber for the ceremonies, dances, clan functions, and social gatherings of men. Activity was so confined around the plaza that everyone knew everyone else's life almost as intimately as his own.

The Corn clan rooms, however, did not face inward toward the plaza but stood behind the Tobacco clan dwelling, facing east where they caught the first rays of the morning sun. The main room of entry contained "curious belongings hung on the wall or thrust above the great ceiling beams—strings of dried [herbs,] . . . gaily painted dolls, blankets, arrows, feathers, and other objects enough to stock a museum."[3] Between the dwelling and the mesa's edge, a second kiva (the Pendete Kiva) had been hollowed out of the rock. At the edge itself, the narrow foot-trail used by residents and visitors alike descended abruptly to the spring and fields below.

1. "Pendete Kiva." Jo
Mora, 1904–1906. (Cline
Library, Special Collec-
tions and Archives
Department, Northern
Arizona University. Neg.
#NAUPH86.1.312)

Nampeyo's home of
the Corn clan dwellings is
behind the stone wall at
the far right of the photo,
facing the Pendete Kiva
and the edge of the mesa.
The top of the trail that
leads to the spring below
can be seen on the left
side of the photo.

Nampeyo was born in one of those Corn clan rooms about
1860. Her parents might have recalled the time only as the
winter when snows blocked the trail to the spring or the summer when blue corn was abundant. The precise date is unknown, because time was not marked off in numbered
segments by a people whose lives were governed by the position of the sun and the rhythm of nature. Whatever the year,
it was what elders call "the old time," when families woke to
the voice of a village crier calling announcements from a rooftop at dawn and went about their tasks barefoot until dark,
setting aside their chores only to prepare for or to celebrate a
ceremony. Except for Navajos, who roamed and ravaged at
will, few outsiders visited the isolated mesas in the mid–1800s.
Residents saw only solitary explorers, such as George C.
Yount;[4] military men on private excursions, such as Dr. P.S.G.
Ten Broeck;[5] or a group of Mormon missionaries led by Jacob

Hamblin.[6] At the time of Nampeyo's birth, no regulatory Hopi agency had been established by the United States government, nor had the concept of a Hopi reservation even been considered.

Nampeyo's father, Quootsva of the Hopi Snake clan,[7] lived with his family in Walpi until he married her mother, White Corn,[8] and moved to her home in Hano. Among both Hopis and Hopi-Tewas, a child was born into the clan of its mother; thus the children of Quootsva and White Corn were all of the Tewa Corn clan. Before the birth of their only daughter, three sons had been born: Polaccaca (who later adopted the name Tom Polacca), about 1849; Kano, about 1854; and Patuntupi (later known as Squash), about 1858. Others may have been conceived, but mortality was high among the newborn.

About 1860, White Corn prepared to give birth to another child. According to custom, one of the whitewashed rooms in the stone house was darkened by hanging rabbitskin quilts at the window openings and the doorway. During her labor, White Corn was comforted and assisted by her mother and her mother's sisters. After the birth, Quootsva's mother was called to cut the umbilical cord, and the paternal grandmother remained with mother and child for twenty days, caring for them in the darkened room. For the mesa people, the transition from womb to world was an unhurried one.

As was customary during confinement, White Corn ate only cornmeal gruel and water boiled with juniper, and every fifth day Quootsva's mother administered a sweatbath by pouring water over a heated stone. The infant was washed frequently, rubbed with fine ash, and given the maternal love innate to Hopi and Tewa women. To supplement this human nurturing, an ear of white corn was placed next to the child to guard it from evil spirits.

Following tradition, all the women of Quootsva's Snake clan gathered in Walpi early on the twentieth day after Nampeyo's birth. With only the stars and moon lighting their way, a quiet procession passed through the middle village to the whitewashed room where White Corn and her baby waited. While a clansman sang, gifts were presented, and each woman in turn dipped an ear of corn into yucca-root suds, then touched it to the infant's head with a prayer and the whisper of a name related to the father's clan. The child was then placed into a new cradleboard together with four ears of corn, wrapped around and around with a sash into secure immobility, and carried from the house by the paternal grandmother as the yellow line of dawn gradually illumined the sky. When the first rays of sun touched the stone house and the gathered clan members, the grandmother said a blessing. Then, speaking to the child, she said, in effect, "You have come out to see the sun," and she gave her a childhood name. Later, when Nampeyo reached puberty, she was given the name "Nung-beh-yong," Tewa for Sand Snake. Outsiders pronounced the name "Nahm-pay-oh" and spelled it phonetically in many ways.

Nampeyo passed her infancy secured within a cradleboard lined with cedar shavings to provide padding and absorption. Oftentimes the board hung from a viga, from which it was swung by grandparents or little brothers passing by. Sometimes White Corn strapped the board to her back, rocking the infant while she worked and sang lullabies. The infant was never left alone, lest, they believed, a spirit of the dead hold the child and the child too would die.

During Nampeyo's lifetime, observers commented that the instinctive affection given to children by the mesa people instilled a security of being and belonging. They rarely heard a child cry or saw one scolded by an adult. Every member of the family in the course of his daily tasks enfolded a newborn, so that it assimilated the activities that would constitute its later life. A mother making pottery would give her child a piece of clay to mold, letting it learn with its own hands what she too had learned in the same way. A father would pick up an infant to his chest while he chanted a song and danced a few steps. Chores, song, and ceremonial dance thus became part of the rhythm of life.

[Nampeyo's] the only daughter. Her brothers and uncles, they can't leave her anywhere alone. They have to watch her close, 'cause it's a cliff, you know. She might be playing around the cliff and she might fall down. As soon as the sun is going down, they get her back to the house. (1982)

During Nampeyo's childhood in the 1860s, no trading posts yet existed near the mesas, so men, women, and children all had to contribute to the chores that provided sustenance for daily life.

> [Nampeyo] likes to go out to get some grass, shake the seeds off, and then tie it with a string and then her mother combs her hair so her hair will be long. That kind of Indian brush won't hurt. (1982)

The child Nampeyo followed her mother about and learned where to dig clay, how to wash impurities from it, how to shape little pots and to fire them. She and White Corn collected beeweed, which they boiled into paint, and they chewed the tough leaves of yucca to make brushes. Making utilitarian pottery was a continuing, time-consuming task, and skill was required to shape the various vessels: cooking pots and large storage jars, stew bowls and water jars, large bowls for mixing batter for piki (tissue-thin blue cornbread that is rolled or folded), seed jars for storing crop seeds for the next year's planting, and cups and ladles.

Small water canteens were fashioned for the men to carry into the fields, but for themselves, women made the cumbersome flat-sided three- to six-gallon canteens that they used to collect water from the spring at the base of the mesa. Tying the pottery jug on her back with a shawl that was then secured around her forehead, the woman made her way down the trail to the spring to wait her turn among her neighbors. Greetings would be exchanged—"lo-la-mi! lo-la-mi![9]—and gossip shared. Shifting the filled jug to her back and bending to support the increased weight, she would trudge slowly, barefoot, back up the narrow trail, stopping occasionally to rest and to let others pass. This daily ritual, passed on from White Corn's mother to White Corn and then to Nampeyo, gradually produced a strange gait, a sort of waddle in which their stocky bodies leaned forward as if into the wind.

Most chores, prayers, and celebrations related to corn, the staple of life. Stacked in storage rooms according to color, it was prepared in countless ways. A corn cob of a dekerneled ear was used to knock the kernels off another dried ear, kernels of different colors that were stewed, popped, roasted, steamed, and ground into meal. White Corn's mother, then White Corn, and eventually Nampeyo herself kneeled before the three flat grinding stones every day. Each of the stones produced a successively finer meal under the mano (handheld stone) that was pushed back and forth to prepare it for gruels, puddings, or batter for piki.

White Corn's house had a separate cooking room, where the child watched and learned how to make the tissue-thin blue piki. Rolled or folded and stacked in layers on a flat basket, piki was a staple with meals, presented as gifts, and given to men preparing for and participating in ceremonies in the kivas. To prepare it, women dexterously scooped a hand into a bowl of blue cornmeal batter and swiped it across a flat hot stone heated by a fire underneath it. The delicate wafer was then quickly folded or rolled and placed on the basket, and without pause, the hand passed again from bowl to hot stone.

As was the practice of all mesa women, White Corn periodically plastered and whitewashed the rooms of her house and kept it in repair. Because hers was the oldest Corn clan dwelling in Hano, it housed clan fetishes and ceremonial objects in a separate chamber safeguarded by the women. In this house of "our oldest mother" of the clan, clan meetings were held to discuss land problems and rituals. Prior to a ceremony, a smoke meeting was held in the clan house to determine the auspicious time for it to begin, which was then announced from a rooftop the following dawn.

> The Corn clan is important. We feed the people. Not food, but we nourish them spiritually. If they come to us, we must be nice to them. (1992)

All this the daughter learned so that she could carry on tradition in the Corn clan dwellings at the top of the trail.

Lands allocated to clans for planting crops lay in the plains surrounding the mesa. Every spring Quootsva carried corn seed saved from the previous crop to the fields and planted it in the Hopi way, dropping several kernels into each deep hole in the sandy soil. As the green leaves sprouted above the earth, he would create windbreaks to shelter the tender growth from burning wind and blowing sand. Without irrigation to water the plants, Quootsva and the other farmers relied solely upon the moisture that collected below ground from the occasional rains that washed over the valleys. Boys of the family spent summer days in the field with their father, chasing crows and burros away from the maturing crop. A burro caught once among the corn had an ear cut off as punishment; if caught again, its other ear was severed.

> *Boys could go out there without knowing that there were snakes that could kill. We go barefooted. We jump from one plant to another without stepping on something. We go way out there and watch over our plants to keep crows and other things that eat them away. That's all we do—sit there all day. (1986)*

All the men descended the mesa toward clan lands in early morning from spring to fall to tend crops and drive sheep from their nighttime corrals. When a rabbit hunt was organized, men and boys ringed an open, scrubby area, gradually closing in on the multitude of long-eared creatures scampering back and forth to elude the boomerangs that were thrown with expert aim.

> *They kill the rabbit. It's easy just to take the skin off and cut the feet and head off and cook it until it is just barely done. Then cut it into pieces just like chicken. Put it in boiling water with white corn ground just like cornmeal. Make a nice stew. Oh, so good. (1982)*

Prairie dogs were also caught for food, and deer were hunted for food and their hides.

> *They don't have no horses and they go on foot and sure enough they bring the deer. They chase it and chase it until they catch up with the deer. They bring the deer and the house just full of jerky. They just making jerky all the time. A long time ago they used to eat prairie dogs. I eat a lot of them. They're big when they are fat. It's just like pork. So white. Better than mutton, better than cow meat. (1982)*

When the air turned cold and snow softened the landscape, Quootsva and the other men descended the pole ladders into the kivas to spin wool and cotton, to weave sashes and fabric for the women's black, one-shouldered woolen garments, and to knit blue leg warmers used by both men and women. They made pahos (prayer sticks) and carved the kachina dolls given to children to teach them the identity and significance of each kachina in their ceremonies.

> *We use cottonwood roots. They're soft enough to carve but don't snap or break off when you carve it.* (1988)

In the kivas, men also participated in the cycle of ceremonies that begin in midwinter with the Soyal, the winter solstice ceremony.[10]

Lengthy, repetitive dances performed in costume and associated with religious and social ceremonies were held in the kiva during winter and on the dirt plaza the remainder of the year. Before, during, and after the dances, homes were opened to members of the extended families, some of whom traveled from distant pueblos. Uninvited guests also were welcomed, including Navajos, who "sprawl into and over the houses and fairly crowd the Hopi women out of their own houses."[11] Folded quilts of rabbit fur or sheepskins served as cushions for the guests, who were served bowls of stew and piki by their hostess.

So days were filled in the old way. Where adults went children always followed, absorbing, listening, and watching in preparation for their future responsibilities. Song was a constant accompaniment. While dancing, grinding corn, rocking a child, driving a flock of sheep into the valley, "All sing as naturally as the bird on the bough."[12]

Youth

"Just like old lady, she makes the potteries." (1982)

Following the traditional male role after marriage, Quootsva slept at White Corn's house in Hano and supplied food and wood for the family, but he returned frequently to his Walpi home, where he had left his religious and personal possessions. There, in the Snake clan household of his mother, he frequently took his meals and shared in the activities and responsibilities of his own clan.

Although it has been said that Quootsva's mother, Nampeyo's Hopi grandmother in Walpi, taught her how to make pottery, this supposition is implausible and has no basis in fact. Probably it derived from a remark in Alexander Stephen's journal dated 1892: "Talking with some Walpi women," he wrote. "The Walpi women (Hopi wu'qti) alone understand well the art of pottery and its decoration. Hano women do make some pottery and decorate it, but it is not beautiful. I called their attention to Nûmpe'yo, but they said she was the exception and had learned her art from the Hopi women."[1]

> Some Hopis say they taught us Tewas in Tewa Village how to make pottery. That's all wrong, of course. Tewas were making pottery back in Tsewageh before they came here. At one time the people on First Mesa had just about stopped making pottery altogether. One of the few people still making pottery then was my great-grandmother, White Corn. She was making pots when most of the Walpis

weren't doing it anymore. Her daughter—that's my grand-
mother on my mother's side—was Nampeyo. ...Nampeyo
improved on her mother's work, and she became very well
known.[2]

The common style of nineteenth-century Hopi pottery, now identified as Polacca Polychrome, had a crackled white surface decorated with stylized birds, flowers, and arabesque motifs. It is not known if White Corn was an expert potter, but the vessels she made influenced Nampeyo's work as she watched and learned. Giving the child a lump of clay, as women did when they were potting for the family, a mother "never said, 'No, no, you're doing it wrong. Make your pot this way.' She simply let the child learn by trial and error and by watching her skillful hands."[3] Nampeyo became adept at pottery-making, and the Hopi women laughed.

Here Nampeyo still a girl, but then she makes pottery. She
heard the Hopis calling her just like old lady, she makes the
potteries. She should be grinding corn or making piki. They
jealous of her. She hears it but she never said nothing and
her mother, too. She felt bad but she never quit making
pottery. Never mind what they say, [she] just go ahead.
(1982)

The term "old lady" has endured, but time has transformed the taunt into a term of affection and respect.

The sharing of song, family chores, clan activities, and the rhythm of traditional life perhaps softened the ridicule in Nampeyo's early years, but the criticism was symptomatic of the tensions existing within the complex interrelationships of all mesa people.[4] The word "jealousy" appears repeatedly in comments about Nampeyo and her clan made to outsiders. Loyalties were governed strictly by adherence to tradition.

All family responsibilities were regulated within the maternal lineage, ruled by the saja (the mother's mother) and the tradition of all grandmothers before her. Until he became old and no longer returned to his own clan home, the grandfather was, in a sense, an outsider, as was the husband of the mother (the father) and the husbands of the daughters. The sons, because they were of the same clan as the mother and their siblings, played an important role in raising their sisters' children. They were the clan uncles who guided them, even though they slept at their wives' homes after marriage.

Extended maternal lineages and clan relationships were equally important, and a second branch of the Corn clan occupied rooms on the northwest corner of the plaza. Members of this Corn clan were latecomers, however, having migrated to Hano between 1870 and 1890. Outwardly the two clans called each other by familiar terms, but "there are times when a degree of coldness, or perhaps of jealousy, keeps us apart."[5]

Not related to lineage or clan were several men's and women's societies and social groups of men who met informally in the kiva nearest their wives' homes. Outside of the complex webs of relationships and loyalties were the other residents, who were "of doubtful friendliness, always capable of hostility, jealousy, and ingratitude."[6] In addition, isolation of White Corn's oldest Corn clan dwellings from the intimacy of the plaza must have intensified a sense of remoteness between her family and other Tewas.

There was also the continuing friction between Hopis and Tewas that originated about 1702, when Hopi chiefs refused to welcome the Tewas after their migration. An antagonism persisted, even though many Hopis and Tewas had intermarried.

During Nampeyo's youth, therefore, despite an outwardly friendly formality, there was underlying resentment by the Tewas toward the Hopi people in general and dissension among the Tewas themselves. Regardless of these tensions, all mesa people tolerated the infiltration of the more aggressive Navajos and all suffered equally from epidemics and drought.

In the early 1860s, when Nampeyo was still a child, no rain fell, fields lay barren, livestock perished, and hundreds of the people died of starvation. The old ones on the mesas said that the people were being punished because they were not in harmony, talked foolishness, and no longer took their traditional ceremonies seriously.

During the famine, the Hopi people had very little to eat, but my grandmother's [Nampeyo's] father was a very good farmer so they always had enough. In those days when

*they ground white corn for special puddings, they would
soak it first and then they would grind it by hand after the
skin of the kernels came off. They put that aside to feed the
chickens. My grandmother couldn't speak Hopi when she
was a little girl because her mother spoke Tewa to her. A
Hopi woman one day asked if she could have the cornskins
that had been set outside the house. She was speaking Hopi
and my grandmother didn't know what she was saying. The
woman pointed to the cornskins and then to a pot she was
carrying. My grandmother nodded and took the pot for the
cornskins. The woman wanted the cornskins to feed her
family. When my grandmother explained to her mother
what she had done, her mother said, "Don't you realize
that you didn't give her nearly what that pot was worth?"
But the woman was willing to give up the pot for the
cornskins to feed her hungry family. (1983)*

Periods of drought produced fearful memories in all mesa
peoples. Hunger, and perhaps Mormon missionaries, taught
them to stock food for future need. Dried corn was stacked
like firewood in storerooms, and storage jars of dried peaches
and other provisions were buried in the dirt floors of the dwellings. From rafters and protruding beams hung strings of beans,
strips of meat, and other foodstuffs drying for use in winter
or time of need. Sustenance for their families, however, was
the only problem they were able to control.

Hopis were defenseless against marauding Navajos, who
infiltrated their lands, grazed their herds, cut scarce wood,
and took water from their springs. The Navajos might leave
one of their children with a mesa family or steal a Hopi or
Tewa child for their own. As F.W. Hodge wrote in his journal
in 1895, "Navajos visit the mesa in droves . . . [and] impose
on the Hopi in no slight degree."[7] Although they had been
incarcerated in Fort Sumner, New Mexico, in 1863, the Navajos had been released five years later to their own reservation, straddling what is now the Arizona/New Mexico border.
Because they required large areas of land for grazing their
sheep and goats, Navajo reservation boundaries were extended
by executive order in 1878, 1880, 1884, 1886, 1900, 1901,
1905, 1907, 1917, and by congressional acts in 1930 and 1933.

Prior to 1882, the Hopis and their lands were not acknowledged or protected by the federal government. As more and

more land was ceded to the Navajos, outside individuals voiced concern about the mesa peoples. Some called for recognition and support, while others advocated their conversion to Christianity and a manner of living more like that of the white man. Initially, a Moqui Pueblo Agency was established at distant Fort Wingate in 1869; it was transferred to Fort Defiance in 1871. The U.S. president and senate appointed Indian agents on the basis of nominations made by religious missionary groups, the goal being to transform the natives into "civilized" beings governed by idealistic men. The Presbyterian Board of Foreign Missions received jurisdiction over the Moqui Agency to nominate qualified men for the post of agent, to supervise them once appointed, and to conduct mission schools under contract with the Bureau of Indian Affairs.

Until a permanent headquarters was built in Keams Canyon in 1902, the Hopis were under the jurisdiction of resident agents who sporadically occupied uninhabitable structures near the mesas, absentee agents who lived at Fort Defiance, or Navajo agents who had no understanding of or interest in the people living on the distant mesas. Intermittently, there was no agent when none could be found to serve that remote area, and those agents who did accept appointment found the Hopis to be an enigma. They lived in a centuries-old manner, shunning change, in isolated villages on the tops of rocky cliffs. They practiced a religion incomprehensible to outsiders. How does one establish authority over such a people?

Different agents wrote summaries and suggested solutions in their annual reports to the commissioner of Indian affairs in Washington D.C. Most complained of the Hopis' impenetrable traditions and recommended removal of the people to a more accessible locality where each family would be allocated a little farm to "Americanize" them. "I was and am still disgusted," wrote John H. Sullivan in 1880, "at their being huddled together, caring little for personal proprieties between sexes, old, young, married, single. . . . Thus housed and homed, the school teacher in his day school and the missionary in his church would find a field in which to work and gather sheaves for the garner."[8] A less charitable motivation had been expressed several years earlier by W.S. Defrees: "All the land will be in a body so we can know what they are doing."[9]

Surely, these agents were reacting to a culture unlike their own and reflecting the teachings of the church that had nominated them. The mesa peoples, living in a present unchanged from the past, were not consulted about proposals to move or "civilize" them. They continued to rise at dawn to face the sun and pray for their people, to listen to the cryer calling news and announcements from a rooftop, to plant their corn, and to follow the traditions of their ancestors from birth until death.

Though they shunned English-speaking intruders who attempted to change their lives, many of the people were multilingual, able to speak Spanish, Navajo, Hopi, and Tewa. With an unusual awareness of the need to communicate with outside authorities, Nampeyo's brother Tom Polacca had learned some English also. His teacher may have been the Mormon missionary Jacob Hamblin, who frequently visited the Hopi villages and who, in his passion to convert the mesa dwellers, would have seen in Polacca an eager, intelligent young man who would serve admirably as his interpreter.

Polacca became a respected Tewa leader and married Okong, whose Tobacco clan dwellings faced the plaza and, in the rear, adjoined the Corn clan rooms. According to custom, he slept at Okong's clan house and provided his share of food and wood, but he remained an active member of the Corn clan household. Official and unofficial visitors sought out "Capitan" Tom, who genuinely welcomed their presence and became their liaison to the seemingly unapproachable people who shunned contact with outsiders.

Among the first to establish a trusting and lasting relationship with Polacca was a young man his own age, Thomas Keam, who opened a trading post that served both Hopis and Navajos in the canyon between First Mesa and Antelope Mesa. When Keam received his license to trade in 1875 he built a stone structure that served as both residence and store, and within a few years, he had added a dozen other buildings: a separate trading post called the "Tusayan Trading Post," storerooms, blacksmith and carpenter shops, stables, quarters for employees and others for guests. The post attracted both Navajos and Hopis, who came by foot, horseback, or burro with goods to trade: hides and sheepskins, blankets and rugs, baskets and pottery. They bartered for flour, sugar, and coffee, and their appetites for such extrinsic goods increased in proportion to the expanding inventory of the post. Calico, dry goods, and groceries were piled on floor-to-ceiling shelves; black iron frying pans, oil lanterns, tin pots and kettles, and coils of rope hanging from the roof beams began to make their way into the natives' homes and lives. Eventually, the bartered goods relieved the people of the chores of weaving cloth, making utilitarian pottery, and grinding their daily corn.

"Keams Canyon," as it came to be called, also became the destination of eastern visitors, most of them government representatives traveling by wagon from Fort Defiance, who stopped for hospitality and information and for Keam's help in fulfilling whatever mission took them to Hopi.[10]

The year that Keam opened his trading post, photographer William Henry Jackson and a small party arrived with camera equipment and pack animals after having photographed the ruins north of the Hopi pueblos. Passing through Keams Canyon, he arrived at First Mesa in August and ascended the trail "and came out finally at the very door of the Capitan's house."[11]

As reported by Jackson's companion E.A. Barber, a special correspondent for the *New York Times*, two men advanced to meet them:

> . . . one, the foremost [Polacca], a bright, fine-looking young fellow, . . . who took off his hat, shook hands, and in broken English, interspersed with Spanish, bade us welcome. . . . After we had shaken hands with several more of the prominent men, . . . our host invited us to enter his house. Following up a ladder to the roof of the second story, and thence to a third by a series of stone steps, we passed through a low aperture into a room on this floor. Here we were bidden to be seated on a raised platform at one side of the room, on which had previously been placed robes made or woven from rabbit skins. . . . Scarcely had we become seated when a beautiful girl approached and placed before us a large mat heaped with pee-kee, or bread. . . . She was of short stature and plump, but not unbecomingly so. Her eyes were al-

2. "Tewa Family on Rooftop." William Henry Jackson, 1875. (Colorado Historical Society. Neg. #WHJ2869)

The young maiden Nampeyo, her brother Tom Polacca, and, presumably, their father, Quootsva, are seated on the rooftop of the Corn clan dwellings, overlooking the plaza of Hano. The ladder protruding from the Monete Kiva can be seen in the center foreground. While the Corn clan dwellings face left to the edge of the mesa, the adjoining Tobacco clan dwellings (the wall behind the family) face directly onto the plaza.

mond shape, coal black, and possessed a voluptuous expression, which made them extremely fascinating. Her hair was arranged in that characteristic Oriental manner, peculiar to her tribe, which denoted her a maid. It was parted in the center, from the front all the way down behind, and put up at the sides in two large puffs, which, although odd to us, nevertheless seemed to enhance her beauty. Her complexion was much lighter than that of her family, and every movement of her head or exquisitely molded hands and arms or

3. "Num-pa-yu, A Moqui maiden of the Pueblo of Tewa." William
Henry Jackson, 1875. (Smithsonian Institution Photo #1841–c)

The first photographs of Nampeyo were taken by Jackson not because
she was a potter but because she was the pretty young sister of Tom
Polacca, Jackson's host and interpreter.

bare little feet was one of faultless grace. . . . We had entered abruptly and awkwardly enough, with our hats unremoved and our garments ragged, travel-stained, and dusty; but on the approach of the modest and beautiful Num-pa-yu—signifying in the Moqui tongue a snake that will not bite—every head was uncovered in a moment, and each of us felt clumsy, dirty, and ashamed of our torn garments and un-shaven faces.[12]

Jackson himself was so attracted to the maiden that he photographed her alone and with members of her family. His photographs show an attractive young woman wearing necklaces and earrings, her hair wrapped into typical Hopi whorls on either side of her head.

Two references suggest that the maidens of Hano had not at that time adopted the decorative hairstyle of their neighbors. In 1852, Dr. P.S.G. Ten Broeck wrote that in the northern town they dressed their hair differently, the unmarried girls wearing their hair long with two knots on each side of the face.[13] In 1886, Victor Mindeleff wrote: "Women wear their hair cut off in front on a line with the mouth and carelessly parted or hanging over the face, the back hair rolled up in a compact queue at the nape of the neck. This uncomely fashion prevails with both matron and maid."[14]

If, indeed, Nampeyo had adopted the decorative Hopi hairstyle before her young Tewa peers, she displayed an early independence in personal expression. The classic photograph of Tom Polacca's sister sitting in a doorway with a sifting basket at her feet predates innumerable photographic images of Nampeyo, the potter, who became a symbol of the Hopi culture.

Marriage

"So one time this Lesso came along." (1982)

Nampeyo matured into a small woman, less than five feet tall, a gentle woman, gracious to outsiders.

> *She was kinda short. Quiet, quiet. She was a quiet lady but she had a good memory.* (1986)

Her father and brothers were ranchers, planting crops and raising cattle and sheep on Corn clan land they called Sand Hill, northeast of Hano. To reach it, they walked northward along the mesa, past peach orchards and fields allotted to other clans. About four miles beyond the village, where the mesa fans out and loses its identity among valleys and rolling hills, lies an expanse of shifting white sand dunes on the northern edge of which flows a spring that gives life to the land. On a low, sloping hillside, the men planted fruit trees—peaches, apricots, apples, and cherries—and fields of corn, beans, squash, and melons. Cattle and sheep grazed on the wild grasses and, later, when the numbers of family members increased, several simple stone houses were built.

> *So one time this Lesso came along. He was working for them. The men are really good workers, her brothers and her uncles. They were all good workers.* (1982)

Lesso[1] was of the Cedarwood clan from Walpi. His Horn clan father, Simo, a respected elder in Walpi, had an un-

4. "Lesho cutting mutton." Adam Clark Vroman, 1901. (Seaver Center, Natural History Museum of Los Angeles County. Photo #V–678)

The only photographs of Lesso that I have found were taken in 1901 by Vroman. This one pictures him cutting mutton; a second one shows him fitting moccasins to the photographer.

traditional, though perhaps not uncommon, background. Simo's grandmother had been stolen from her family when she was a child by Navajos who raised her as their own. She married a Navajo and gave birth to two daughters, who, when they were of age, shared the same Navajo husband. The elder daughter and her son Simo returned to her Horn clan people in Walpi when Simo was about five years old. He eventually married a woman of the Cedarwood clan who bore him a son, Lesso, and she died when Lesso was still a child. Because the Horn clan relationship had passed unbroken from the grandmother to mother to Simo, his Navajo blood was irrelevant when he was named Horn clan chief and the kikmungwi (town chief) of Walpi.

Lesso courted Nampeyo and became her husband through the lengthy marital tradition of both Hopis and Tewas. As the transition from womb to outside world was unhurried, so the joining of man and wife took time. Nampeyo's wedding clothes would have been woven in the kiva by Lesso and his uncles, who would also have made her white deerskin leggings and moccasins. When the propitious time for the wedding was set, Nampeyo began grinding corn to present to her husband's family, and at his house (or perhaps, because his mother had died, at the home of a female clan relative), she kneeled to the grinding stones again to grind more corn into meal. Puddings were made and buried in fire-pits to cook overnight. The hands of female relatives swept across hot stones to make piki to accompany the feasts, and sheep were slaughtered by the men, who cooked mutton and hominy stew over outdoor fires. Each day, the extended family members gathered in a circle to sit on blankets and sheepskins on the floor, passing communal bowls of stew, puddings, dried peaches, and watermelons that had been preserved in sand from summer. They feasted, laughed, and shared stories in the conviviality of the occasion.

On one of the last evenings of the days-long celebration, with the floor cleared and relatives seated around one of the rooms of the Cedarwood clan, Nampeyo, like every bride before her, was ceremonially dressed by one of Lesso's female relatives. First were the robes woven in the kiva: the tubelike black woolen manta, a narrow red-and-black sash over which a wider white sash with tassels at each end wrapped around her waist, and heavy oblong white cotton robes that were placed around her shoulders, one of which would be kept for her burial to carry her back to the underworld. Her legs were wrapped with fine white deerskins and white moccasins were placed on her feet. Finally, her hair was combed out into the two long twists of a married woman, to fall over both shoulders, and fine white powder was dusted on her face.

Lesso was then seated with Nampeyo in the middle of the room, where they received an emotional blessing and advice from each elder of the clan: Be kind to each other; be good to your children; don't forget what your parents have taught you.

The old ones teach the men to take care of the women who keep the clan going. The men have work to do. They have to provide like birds to the nest. The wedding is a lesson of the clan to the young people. (1988)

5. "Nampeyo carrying an olla." Adam Clark Vroman, 1901. (The Southwest Museum, Los Angeles. Photo #N22764.)

Nampeyo posed for Vroman inside her house with the typical canteen carried by women to obtain water from the spring below the mesa.

After each elder had given his or her advice, Lesso and Nampeyo, who by then resembled a stocky white pyramid in her heavy robes and thick-wrapped legs, led a procession of relatives back to her home in Hano for more feasting. There, her wedding robes were removed and stored for other ceremonies in her life. In the July following her marriage, Nampeyo dressed as a bride once again to make her appearance with similarly dressed young women who had married during that year at the Niman ceremony, the last dance of the kachinas before departing for the San Francisco Peaks. For the last time in their lives, she and the other brides were presented with carved cottonwood kachina dolls by the kachina dancers, signifying the end of their childhood.

When, after their marriage, Lesso moved into the stone house at the top of the trail, he became Nampeyo's lifelong companion and the father of six children of whom we know.[2] In 1878, Indian Agent Wm. R. Mateer included the couple in "a complete list of all heads of families, and individual Indians entitled to receive supplies."[3] On First Mesa, Mateer counted 277 residents in Walpi; 116 in Sichomovi; and 143 in Hano, including "Pu-lac-ca" with one woman and one girl child, and "Lesh-sho" with one woman.[4]

Because his Cedarwood clan mother had died when he was young, Lesso may have remained at Nampeyo's home,[5] not sharing time, as was customary, with the family in which he had been raised, for his father had remarried into a different clan. He worked at the ranch with Nampeyo's father and brothers, spun wool and wove Nampeyo's garments, and performed all traditional male duties. As the youngest woman of the household, Nampeyo fulfilled the customary female tasks: grinding corn, carrying water from the spring below, digging clay for the time-consuming task of making utilitarian and decorated pottery.

Ancient sherds and ancestral vessels were familiar to all mesa residents: black-on-white ware of the ancient ones, black-on-red of Kayenta, black-on-yellow of Awatovi and Jeddito, and the subsequent polychromes of Sikyatki, San Bernardo, and Payupki. Families not only possessed heirlooms of the saja and the sajas before her but also knew the ruins of pre-historic villages where abandoned pots and sherds permeated the ground. Exposed by wind and heavy rains, they were relics of those who had moved on or had been destroyed by enemy violence. Many abandoned village sites, including Awatovi, dotted Antelope Mesa to the east; others were scattered throughout the Hopi area. The crumbled walls of Sikyatki lay in a rise on the east base of First Mesa, where sheep grazed and cornfields grew, only three miles from Hano. Above Sikyatki at the mesa's edge, two rocky cones marked its location. The short way to reach the ruin was by a steep path down, but an easier although longer trail followed the base of the mesa from the spring northward.

"When I first began to paint," Nampeyo told Ruth Bunzel through an interpreter in the 1920s, "I used to go to the ancient village and pick up pieces of pottery and copy the designs. That is how I learned to paint. But now I just close my eyes and see designs and I paint them."[6]

When did Nampeyo depart from the Zuni-style decoration of Polacca Polychrome to incorporate those prehistoric designs in her work? No Sikyatki influence was yet in evidence in the massive collections of unsigned Hopi ceramics made during the early years of her marriage, 1879 and the early 1880s. The insatiable appetite for ethnologic objects during those years, however, no doubt disrupted the natural development not only of her work but also that of other potters. Collectors, the National Museum[7] primarily, annually swept up all significant specimens, both modern and ancient, "to illustrate the manner, customs, habits, and arts, of a people . . . whose utter extinction would seem to be certain at no very distant day."[8]

John Wesley Powell,[9] first director of the Smithsonian's Bureau of Ethnology, believed that its most important task was research and compilation of information about native peoples. Working under Spencer F. Baird, secretary of the Smithsonian, who believed that collections of material culture were essential, Powell focused on the Southwest, where ancient cultures remained relatively unchanged by outsiders. They reasoned that native people were soon to become extinct, so an immediate collection of artifacts should be made for future anthropological study.

From 1879 through the following decade, literally tons of domestic clothing, basketry, kachina dolls, toys, religious objects, blankets, looms, cradleboards, gourds, dance masks, stone implements, and pottery were obtained from village households and excavated sites in both the Zuni and Hopi regions to be sent to Washington.[10] The motive behind this compulsive acquisitiveness could not have been understood by the people from whom these familiar objects were taken.

In 1879, under the direction of James Stevenson, the first collecting expedition amassed nearly two thousand specimens: kachina dolls, water jugs and jars, bowls, cooking vessels, ladles, baskets, and other domestic implements. In his catalog of the collection, Stevenson described Hopi pottery as bearing so strong a resemblance to that of Zuni that it was almost impossible to distinguish the two if mingled. Comparing modern to ancient pottery specimens, he discerned no attempts by modern potters to imitate exact forms or the ceramic designs of their predecessors.[11]

Stevenson directed other expeditions to the area in 1880 and 1881, gathering a total of forty-nine hundred specimens the latter year, of which Powell reported that material secured from Hopi alone weighed twelve thousand pounds. Included were vessels of atypical shape and decoration, the origin of which the Hopis said they had no knowledge. Powell surmised that these were vessels from Awatovi, because those ruins had revealed quantities of broken pottery similar in form and decoration.[12]

The footpath carved into the rocky cliff as a defense against Spanish aggression three centuries earlier was a hindrance to white men and their horses attempting to reach villages on the top of the mesa. Over time, a horse trail was worn into softer ground along a less precipitous route. That too became an obstacle in 1879, when representatives of the National Museum began a decade of transporting goods to barter in the villages above and descending with the abundance of specimens to be carried away.

To ease the problem, the horse trail was widened during

the early 1880s to allow access for wagons.[13] Under supervision of "an American,"[14] blasting tore chunks of rock from the cliff to achieve a more passable ascent. Work at the top destroyed the Pendete Kiva at the cliff's edge, and protesting elders predicted dire calamity from the sacrilege. To provide residents with a new kiva, more blasting created a subterranean chamber closer to Nampeyo's house that would be finished by clansmen. While the dust billowed and the rock foundation shook, the family must have taken refuge at their Sand Hill ranch.

Tracks for the Atlantic and Pacific Railroad (later purchased by the Atchison, Topeka and Santa Fe Railway) laid from New Mexico across northern Arizona in the early 1880s made the mesas more accessible. Passengers could disembark at either Holbrook or Winslow, where livery stables provided a driver and wagon, camping gear, and necessary provisions. The parties then traveled north over wagon ruts and possible washouts in arroyos, through barren country of intense dry heat in the summer and localized torrential rain showers in the fall, with at least one overnight stop along the way. Anthropologists, artists, photographers, missionaries, and eventually curious tourists all made their way to the mesas to study, to paint, to photograph, to convert, to peer at the people and their customs, and to purchase souvenirs of their visit.

The intensified interest concentrated on these previously isolated people and the conflicting policies concerning them forced the government to establish the "Moqui Reserve."[15] On December 4, 1882, President Chester A. Arthur signed an executive order describing the boundaries:

> It is hereby ordered that the tract of country in the Territory of Arizona lying and being within the following-described boundaries, viz, beginning on the one hundred and tenth degree of longitude west from Greenwich, at a point 36 degrees and 30 minutes north, thence due west to the one hundred and eleventh degree of longitude west, thence due south to a point of longitude 35 degrees and 30 minutes north, thence due east to the one hundred and tenth degree of longitude, and thence due north to place of beginning, be, and the same is hereby, withdrawn from settlement and sale, and set apart for the use and occupancy

of the Moqui and such other Indians as the Secretary of the Interior may see fit to settle thereon.[16]

The federal government did not consult with the Hopi people about this order or the boundaries described; there was no consideration of their rights and their needs. Conflicts concerning the area established "for the Moqui and such other Indians as the Secretary of the Interior may see fit to settle thereon" have persisted to the present day, with Navajo claims on the land unresolved after more than a century.

Yet, at the time, the order was deemed of so little importance that the absentee Indian agent, D. M. Riordan, wrote from Fort Defiance to the commissioner of Indian affairs one year after the reservation was established, "As for the Moquis Pueblo reservation although I understand from current rumor that there is such a thing, I have no authoritative information that there is; neither from the Department nor from any offices of the Government. Nor that I have anything to do with it."[17]

Although the order recognized the Hopi people by setting boundaries on land for their occupancy, the Bureau of Ethnology continued its activities, collecting specimens and data that would illustrate their culture, past and present. In the fall of 1882, Director Powell sent Victor and Cosmos Mindeleff to the mesas to survey the seven villages and the peripheral ruins. They drew architectural plans and sketches of construction details and took photographs for the purpose of gathering data for the construction of an accurate, large-scale model of the Hopi area for the National Museum. They observed that the large roofing timbers of several of the kivas had been beams scavenged from old Spanish churches. The Mindeleffs also collected pottery and sherds from ruins and compiled mythological and historical information, obtained from Alexander Stephen, for their report.[18]

During these undertakings, Victor received a further directive from Powell to make still another collection of material goods from Hopi. The party, which included Frank Hamilton Cushing, an anthropologist of the Bureau of Ethnology working at Zuni, and Tom Polacca, acting as interpreter, was instructed to "'clean out' Oraibe—ethnologically speaking."[19] When they arrived in Oraibi, the group was first welcomed, then threatened by the elders when the purpose of the visit became known.[20] Before their departure, however, they had bartered with women of the pueblo and carried away more than two hundred specimens.[21]

From the three villages on Second Mesa, Mindeleff obtained twelve hundred more objects, of which 150 were ancient pottery. Powell reported that those vessels were the most valuable items in the collection, as such specimens were rare and highly prized by the people.[22]

Stevenson made several more trips to Zuni and Hopi, collecting sacred and household objects as well as obtaining ethnologic information. During the several months he spent among the Hopi villages in 1885 and 1886, he succeeded in making "a large collection of rare objects, all of which were selected with special reference to their anthropologic importance."[23]

Transporting specimens from isolated pueblos to Washington was more difficult than the collecting itself. Lumber and materials for building crates were transported to the site, the specimens packed in wool, and the crates hauled by wagon. After completion of the railroad through Arizona in the early 1880s, crates were transferred to rail cars for their final journey to Washington, where, frequently, they were left outside the Smithsonian building until space could be found to store them. Damaged items were simply discarded, because the museum staff was overwhelmed with the rapid pace of the bureau's collecting.

While the National Museum was acquiring these massive collections, visitors and military men who frequented the mesas also carried away numerous "souvenirs." Lt. John G. Bourke, on leave in 1880 and 1881 to record the customs of Indians of the Southwest, traveled to Hopi to witness the Snake Dance. While there, Bourke added to his collection begun thirteen years earlier of native pottery, silverware, weapons, domestic fabrics, utensils, and ancient vessels. The baskets that he acquired "used in the snake dance of the Moquis [are] so quaint and beautiful that no lady need be ashamed to have them on the walls of her parlor."[24] Shipped to his rooms at army headquarters in Omaha, crates also contained kachina dolls, blankets and rugs, pipes and stone implements—a massive haul of "treasures which would have made the heart of an ethnologist jump with joy."[25]

In addition to the extensive collection of fine specimens he kept for himself, Thomas Keam also made substantial collections for museums in Europe and the United States. In 1881, under contract with the Bureau of Ethnology, Keam secured forty thousand pounds of "characteristic pottery from the Moquis" to be exchanged by the government for relics and curiosities from foreign countries for display in the National Museum.[26]

Directly and indirectly, the question of the authenticity of specimens of ancient ware began to be raised. As early as 1882, William H. Holmes wrote in an article, "Pottery of the Ancient Pueblos," that ancient vessels could be culled from ruins, caves, cliff houses, and burial sites, as well as acquired from the Indians themselves. The country around Moqui, he said, had been ransacked and many valuable specimens removed, but it seemed unaccountable to him that such a great number of ancient vessels should still be preserved.[27]

A less than scholarly but pragmatic answer to Holmes's concern appeared in a story in the *New York Tribune* in 1882:

> One touch of nature makes all mankind and the Indian akin
> . . . the wonderful facility with which he takes advantage of
> the antiquarian craze. Ancient Indian pottery has been
> sought after through the past few years with great zeal. The
> custom of the average tourist, in seizing upon everything in
> the way of pottery that bears the semblance of age, has
> made such a demand for "prehistoric" wares that the inge-
> nious mind of the native has led him to devise means of
> gratifying the aesthetic longings of his cultured brother. The
> method is simple. The Indian just manufactures it in propor-
> tion to the wants of the trade.[28]

Initially, Baird and Powell had selected the relatively isolated mesas from which to make collections because of the unchanging Hopi way of life. The intrusion of collecting, however, initiated changes by its very activity. Encouraged by the outsiders to give up ancestral vessels, everyday utensils, and commonplace objects, the people could not have understood that these possessions were to be stored in a museum as material examples of a culture soon to become "extinct." If the white men wanted "things," they must have reasoned, why not make more of the objects for which they paid the highest price: pottery in the ancient style.

Consider a woman who had always coiled and fired jars painted with Zuni-style decoration and plain, functional vessels for family use. Museum representatives visit her stone home and cast covetous eyes on an ancestral piece that had always been there, during her mother's lifetime and her grandmother's and even before that. The men offer her more cloth and flour for her ancient family jar than for the new one she is making with her own hands, so after they leave, she attempts to duplicate the ancient pot. Her first efforts may not have been successful, but by the time the collectors visit again, she and many of her neighbors are producing pottery of similar character.

The intrusive collection of material culture affected every household in seven villages on all three mesas. In the federal census of 1890, 365 women stated that their "Occupation" was "Potter." During that decade of acquisition, Hopi women thought beyond their traditional roles of saja and clanswoman to that of craftswoman, fashioning decorative vessels to barter with white men. By the turn of the century when the Smithsonian's focus had turned elsewhere, other regional institutions began making collections on a lesser scale. When their pieces were no longer in demand, few women persisted with their "occupations"; they returned to traditional roles in the household, of which making utilitarian vessels was merely a customary chore. In the 1900 federal census, only Nampeyo and one other woman called themselves a "Potter."

As Nampeyo continued shaping the clay, her work became the paradigm of a new art form, the revival of ancient pottery shapes and designs. But it was her brother's amicable relationship with outsiders that attracted their attention to her work. They came seeking Tom Polacca, Tewa leader and interpreter, and left carrying vessels made by his sister, Nampeyo.

Schools

"You will forget how to make it warm." (1988)

Nothing is known about Nampeyo's early pottery. In the 1880s, she was one of many unknown potters making vessels that she hoped could be bartered to museum representatives. She dug her clay and refined it, collected beeweed and made her paint, and from sherds that could be found around the mesa and in nearby ruins, she borrowed designs of ancient styles. To obtain water for her pottery-making and for family use, she descended the trail with a heavy canteen secured to her back, indistinguishable in her black manta from all the other women performing the same task. After filling the bulky vessel at the spring, she readjusted the strap supporting the canteen around her forehead and, leaning forward, carried the heavy burden back up the cliffside.

> *Sometimes she would go four times in one day with a canteen to Coyote Spring to get water. She had two big water jars in her house that were coated with pitch, inside and out, where she kept all the water. It stayed so cold. When I think about all the water I use to make my pottery, it's hard to think that she had to carry all hers from below.* (1990)

During that decade of anonymity, Nampeyo bore three children into her Corn clan, sequestered each time in a darkened room for twenty days. Her eldest daughter, Quinchawa, was born about 1884 and two sons followed: Kaloakuno a year or two later and Komaletiwa about 1887. In the Tobacco clan dwellings next door, Tom Polacca's wife, Okong, bore three children also: a girl about 1878, and two boys about 1883 and 1886. While Nampeyo continued to live within Corn clan tradition, Polacca, with his more expansive relationship with outsiders, embraced not only nontraditional customs but Christianity as well. During early missionary efforts of the Mormons, he had accepted the teachings of the Church of Jesus Christ of Latter-day Saints, apparently converted by the charismatic Jacob Hamblin during one of his visits to the Hopi mesas.

Perhaps in emulation of the white man, perhaps with foresight of the future, Polacca built the first house off the mesa on a small hill near the spring. It was constructed in Mexican style with an enclosed courtyard and portico, walls nearly two feet thick, and a board ceiling in the main living room. Beneath the projecting roof in the courtyard he improvised tables from boxes and boards, around which his frequent white guests sat on more boxes, a few chairs, and upturned baskets and pails. While residents on the mesa offered visitors mutton stew and piki, Polacca served roasted chicken, potted ham and beef, bread and grape jam, and coffee boiled on a stove. Apart from Keam's quarters, Polacca's house provided the sole oasis of rest and nourishment for men and their horses before they resumed their journeys, traveling on or up to the villages. Like many contemporary residents of Hopi, Polacca and his family lived in two houses, enjoying the comforts and visitors below and moving to the mesa house above for ceremonies and clan activities.

> Tewas right from the start, they try to get along with the government and different people. The Hopis hold back, hold onto one chief, the Hopi chief. Everything he say, they say. That's it. Nobody say a word. They too far backward. Polacca, he was the first one to negotiate with white people when government people came in. He's a man of everything, I think.[1] (1986)

Polacca's comfortable relationship with outsiders and his concern about the future of his own children and Nampeyo's, of whom he was a Corn clan uncle, led him to support Thomas Keam's advocacy for schools. Though the Tewas listened, the Hopis rejected this latest proposed interference into their lives.

The old ones say you lose traditions, you will forget how to make it warm. Some day you will be planting corn with gloves on. (1988)

To implement the establishment of a school, in 1887 Keam rented and later sold his holdings in the canyon to the federal government and moved his trading post to a new site on the main wagon road just west of the entrance to the canyon. The building was constructed of corrugated metal painted red, and a cellar was dug for storage of supplies. On a knoll opposite from which he could overlook the new post, corrals, the wagon road, and the hills beyond, Keam built his residence. The house, too, was built over a cellar for the security of his increasing and valuable collection of artifacts.[2]

After the government acquired Keam's holdings, the school's first superintendent, James Gallaher, arrived in the canyon in May of 1887 to confront the difficult task of converting the empty buildings into offices, classrooms, and living quarters. By September he reported to the commissioner of Indian affairs that he had been promised fifty-six children from First Mesa, forty from Second Mesa, and a few from Oraibi.

The school was opened on October 3, 1887, with thirty-one boys and nineteen girls in attendance, but after two weeks only a dozen children remained. On October 15, Thomas Keam visited each village to inquire why the other children had left, a task he was to undertake frequently to convince families of the importance of educating their young. The answer from parents was always the same: Children belong at home, where they can participate in the continuing cycle of traditional ceremonies, as had their parents and grandparents and all generations before them.

Instead of acknowledging the problem to his superiors, and perhaps to enhance his own position, Superintendent Gallaher stated in his official report at the end of the year that the school in Keams Canyon was a complete success. In 1889, S.C. Baker succeeded Gallaher; in 1890, Ralph P. Collins succeeded Baker; in 1893, another superintendent took charge; in 1895, still another; and in 1896 Collins returned. Until 1899, when the roles of school superintendent and Indian agent were combined into one resident position in Keams Canyon, the numerous superintendents functioned inefficiently and with difficulty under the administration of the agent at Fort Defiance, while attempting to keep their students in a school of which most of the parents disapproved.

Imagine the children—who had played without modesty of clothing most of the year, whose complex language was unwritten, whose oral traditions were passed from generation to generation, whose spiritual guidance was received from myriad masked kachinas—dressed in restrictive clothing, made to sit still in chairs to which they were unaccustomed, being taught in a language incomprehensible to them. They fled, shedding the strange clothing as they ran. School employees pursued them, seeking them out in the storage areas of their homes where their mothers had hidden them. When the runaways were found and taken back, "the women set up howls and lamentations which would put the coyote of the desert to shame."[3] The task of educating unwilling children who were protected by their resolute parents compounded tensions between the people and government representatives.

Official written reports required of those in the field at that time were rarely objective. Soaring hyperbole or abject depression often colored them with subjective expression. On September 8, 1890, Indian Agent C.E. Vandever sent a laconic appraisal of the situation to Governor Bradford L. Prince of New Mexico: "At Keams Canyon a school established in 1887 is not markedly successful."[4] Contradicting Vandever's terse judgment, Brevet Major General A. D. McCook reported in the same year that the school was in successful operation: The children were neat, clean, and well fed and would leave the school "carrying with them an education and habits of life far superior to any they had heretofore enjoyed, and no one can fail to believe, or to hope at least, that the 103 children now present in the school, returning to their homes imbued with another and better civilization, will produce much good. . . . I am glad to report that 44 of the pupils are from

6. "Tom Polaccaca, Tewa Indian." Unknown, 1890. (Smithsonian Institution Photo #1803–c)

Polaccaca was the anglicized spelling of his Tewa name. Tom Polacca was the adopted name of Nampeyo's remarkable brother. This portrait was taken when he traveled to Washington D.C. with four Hopi chiefs to meet with the commissioner of Indian affairs about the intrusion of Navajos onto Hopi lands.

Areibe [Oraibi] village and not the least comely of the pupils gathered there."[5]

In that same year, Keam wrote a series of letters to the commissioner of Indian affairs stating that "we succeeded in getting three boys to come, which is all the attendance at present"[6] and that "the Oraibis have not sent a child yet."[7]

The purpose of Keam's letters to the commissioner was to ask permission for five Hopi and Tewa leaders to travel to Washington to discuss the continuing problem of encroachment on their lands by the Navajos. Concerned that the importance of schooling was not understood by the elders, he suggested an exchange of promises between the government and the chiefs: The government would pay expenses for the chiefs to travel to Washington so that their grievances against the Navajos would be heard; the chiefs in turn would guarantee to fill the school with children. After voluminous correspondence with Keam, the commissioner approved the proposed plan.

Accompanied by Thomas Keam and Indian Agent C.E. Vandever, the five chiefs—Lesso's father, Simo of Walpi; Tom Polacca of Hano; Anawita of Sichomovi; Honani of Shongopovi; and Lololami of Oraibi—traveled to Washington, where they met on June 27, 1890, with Commissioner T.J. Morgan. The transcript of the meeting provided by Morgan's office reported a simplistic exchange of ideas. The chiefs expressed their thanks to the commissioner for allowing them to meet with him in Washington and described their lives on the mesas. "My people told me to see everything, to find out how Americans live, whether there are many of them &c. I have seen wonderful things. What Indians want most is green grass," the transcript quoted Honani as saying. The commissioner responded to the brief statements given by the chiefs that, if their children would go to school and stay, "then your girls would learn to wash, iron, keep house, and your boys would learn farming, blacksmithing, carpentoring [sic] &c., they could learn to do just as well as white children do . . . and so far as I can I will help those who [move] down from the mesa. I cannot do very much, but I will do what I can."[8] There is no reference in the transcript to the question of land boundaries and only minor mention of the Hopis' grievances against Navajo aggression.

The consequences of the Washington meeting could not have been more explosive, particularly in Oraibi on Third Mesa, the most conservative of the villages. The people there imprisoned their chief, Lololami, in a kiva for encouraging the villagers to send their children to the Keams Canyon school. Soldiers were sent to Oraibi to release the chief, but opposition to the school continued and the villagers threatened to fight before any children were taken.

Anger against outside interference erupted when, without explanation, surveyors began to place stakes throughout the lands in the government's effort to break up centuries-old clan holdings. The Oraibis pulled up the stakes, destroyed survey markers, and threatened to raid the Keams Canyon school. A small detachment of soldiers was sent to Oraibi on June 21, 1891, to arrest the leaders of the resistance, but they were confronted by about fifty hostile villagers, armed and stationed behind a barricade. The soldiers retreated and called for a stronger force with Hotchkiss guns.

On July 1, four troops of cavalry with two Hotchkiss guns left Keams Canyon with Keam acting as guide and interpreter. They marched across the hot plains, past the base of First Mesa, and made camp the first night at a spring near Mishongnovi at the base of Second Mesa. Early the following morning, they moved on to Oraibi, confronted the hostile villagers, and arrested the war chief and ten other leaders. Lt. Col. H.C. Corbin, commander of the troops, demanded the people's obedience to their chief, Lololami, and ordered the guns to be fired in a demonstration of strength. With their eleven prisoners, the troops returned to their camp at Second Mesa for the night and to Keams Canyon the following day. Corbin subsequently wrote in his report that he had ordered a contingent of the troops to take the prisoners to Fort Wingate and that the campaign was a complete success "without the loss of a single man."[9]

The Oraibi skirmish was only the first of several forays by the military to make the people capitulate. Temporarily, it restored peace. In 1894, in a gesture of compromise, the government started two day schools where children could be educated closer to their homes: one in Oraibi and the other in a little stone building at the base of First Mesa.

> At that time my great uncle [Polacca] was policeman at Keams Canyon. For anything they sent him out to people because he is the kind that was never afraid to do anything they ask him. When the Hopi chief refused to sign for the school, he was disgusted. He said, "Never mind about those chiefs. I'll write my signature okay." That's what happened. That's why Polacca Day School named after him. Then when everything is over, Hopis begin to wake up. They feel hurt, but too late. (1986)

Despite the conflict, Nampeyo, like the other Tewas, agreed to send her children to be educated, and Quinchawa would have been the first to go. Because she was of school age before the day school in Polacca had opened, she was sent to board at the Moqui Training School in Keams Canyon. When she returned home at the end of her first year, she had been renamed

Annie Lesso by school authorities. She could speak hesitant English, and like the other children, she was dressed in non-traditional clothing. Pretty and quiet like her mother, Annie was not estranged from her traditional background by schooling or her absences from home. After completing her compulsory education, she returned to the Corn clan dwellings to work alongside Nampeyo making pottery for outsiders to buy. When she was about sixteen years old, Annie married Okong's nephew, Ipwantiwa, of the Tobacco clan next door. Ipwantiwa had been given the name Willie in school and the surname Healing, the English pronunciation of his mother's name, Heli.

Nampeyo's sons, Kaloakuno and Komaletiwa, may have started school in the Polacca Day School, hiking down the trail in front of their home each day to the stone schoolhouse below. When authorities anglicized Hopi and Tewa names, all of Nampeyo's children were given their father's name, Lesso, as a surname. Komaletiwa became William; Kaloakuno's anglicized name has been forgotten by the family members with whom I spoke.

Although some families, most of them Tewa, adapted to the new authority in their lives, compulsory education became another divisive issue on the mesas, further alienating Hopis from Tewas, conservatives from progressives, the people from government representatives. Hopi villagers blamed Tom Polacca as the perpetrator.

Two Anthropologists

"Nümpe'yo, the distinguished Tewa potter."
   —Hopi Journal of Alexander M. Stephen

Alexander Stephen, who took up residence in Keams Canyon about 1880, was one of several pioneer anthropologists working among Southwest Indian cultures during that era. He studied the Navajos and learned to speak their language, the common language with which he and Thomas Keam, Zunis, Hopis, Tewas, and Navajos communicated. Desiring to study the mesa people more closely, Stephen moved to the top of First Mesa about 1890, where he lived intermittently in the Tobacco clan dwellings in Hano and in other clan houses in Sichomovi and Walpi. For occasional respite from the confining mesa life, he descended to Polacca's house below.

Stephen began to learn the complex spoken Hopi language and was accepted into community and ceremonial life.[1] He recorded his experiences in a daily journal that became a detailed description of the elaborate ceremonies and an intimate commentary on the lives of the mesa people. His few descriptions of Nampeyo and her family may be the only written observations of their private lives.

Stephen watched Nampeyo sitting in front of a fire, stirring with a bundle of straight greasewood a pot of dry, coarse, bluish meal for ceremonial use.[2] He described Lesso in the white mask of a Navajo Yebichai, dancing the part of grandfather in a kachina dance with gestures and springy steps that suggested a jig.[3] Nampeyo's father, Quootsva (spelled "Kuichve" by Stephen), who joined Stephen for a smoke, grumbled that his old wife, White Corn, went too often to Keams Canyon when she should be in the fields husking corn.[4] Criticizing his son-in-law, Quootsva called Lesso "lazy," a term of rebuke among the Hopis.[5]

In addition to ceremonial activities and personal vignettes, Stephen recorded the process of firing pottery with dung and coal, with corncobs and bones sometimes added to the fire.[6] Near a spring in the foothills, Stephen helped a woman and her husband prospect for coal with which to fire some pottery that she had made and decorated. Indicating that potters were producing revival pottery in early 1893, the date of his diary entry, he wrote, "She does not approach Nümpe'yo, the distinguished Tewa potter, in artistic skill. . . . Like Nümpe'yo she tells me she makes her designs after some she has seen on ancient ware, but knows nothing of their significance."[7]

Stephen was known as a careful recorder and was respected by other researchers in the field. He was asked frequently to provide them with information, which they rewrote under their own names, not always with acknowledgment to their source. Because his empirical studies were made without a sponsor, however, he was overshadowed by those working for established institutions, who were ensured of publication and recognition by the scientific community. Stephen's journals were not published until 1936, and then in edited form.

Long before that time, one of Stephen's contemporaries denigrated Stephen's copious written observations and, with a mass of published writings about Hopi ceremonials, many based on Stephen's notes, established himself as the authority on Hopi studies. Jesse Walter Fewkes also disregarded the potters who had created a revival pottery style and credited the revival to his own excavation of Sikyatki in 1895. He criticized Nampeyo by name for cleverly copying those vessels that he unearthed, implying that they were being sold as the ancient ware itself.

Fewkes was a dominant, verbose figure who aroused strong, disparate feelings among his peers.[8] He was an indefatigable worker with a photographic memory, but his compulsive need to publish scattered his attention and led him to reconstruct notes made by others. His frequent self-contradictions, a propensity for disparaging the work of others, and a compulsion to prove his own preconceived theories compromised many of his findings.

Fewkes graduated in zoology from Harvard University and continued his studies at the University of Leipzig. He worked in several marine laboratories before accepting a position in Harvard's Museum of Comparative Zoology. After nine years, he was denied reappointment by the director because, as was common throughout his career, he had used another worker's material without acknowledgment. Unemployed and having recently become a widower, he was asked by Mrs. Mary Hemenway, a wealthy Boston benefactress and the mother of one of his Harvard classmates, to salvage a disappointing anthropological expedition to Zuni that she had sponsored.

The expedition, directed by Frank Hamilton Cushing, was attempting to trace the origins of the Zuni culture, but Cushing's fragile health and lack of administrative skills impaired the project. The group disbanded within two years with little descriptive data of their archaeological fieldwork.

Enthusiastic to continue the project but changing the focus from Zuni origins to the culture itself, Mrs. Hemenway supplied Fewkes with a gramophone and wax discs to record ceremonies and sent him to Zuni in 1890. His lack of understanding of the Pueblo people and his withdrawn demeanor in the aspects of fieldwork caused other scientists in the field to question his competence. Nevertheless, Fewkes retained Mrs. Hemenway's confidence, and in 1891 he turned his attention to the Hopi people when she asked him to direct a second expedition.

Upon his arrival at First Mesa, he found Alexander Stephen living among the villagers, compiling a journal of their activities. Striving to assimilate the complex Hopi culture as rapidly as possible, Fewkes enlisted Stephen to record details of the ceremonies for him. As a consequence of Stephen's cooperation, Fewkes wrote authoritative reports of what he and Stephen witnessed together and what Stephen alone observed and recorded during Fewkes's absences.

Fewkes's first trip to the mesa introduced him to the volatile relationship between the federal government and Hopi elders. Whether he was merely an observer or an active participant in the military campaign against the Oraibi villagers is not clear, either from his reports or those of others. On July 2, 1891, Fewkes wrote an impassioned letter to Mrs. Hemenway, explaining that the Oraibis did not want to send their children to a school in which their traditional beliefs would be supplanted by those of white men. He asked, "Why cannot they be left alone?"[9] and he described the troops that "marched through our place for the seat of war" with two Hotchkiss guns.[10] "At one time we were a little anxious in as much as we were fifteen miles nearer the hostiles than any White men for four days, but during that time we went on with our studies visiting our friends daily and witnessing their ceremonials."[11]

Thirty years later, in an article written for the *American Anthropologist*, Fewkes recalled that he had been asked to join the party as it passed the mesa with "four" Hotchkiss guns, and in describing the events that unfolded in Oraibi, he placed himself near Colonel Corbin, whom he called "Major" Corbin, while the commander negotiated with the Oraibi chief.[12]

When Fewkes returned to Boston after his first visit to Hopi, he reported his field activities to his wealthy patron, and his description of Keam's personal collection of Hopi artifacts produced a strong reaction in Mrs. Hemenway. Desirous of housing such a collection in a museum adjoining her home, Mrs. Hemenway authorized Fewkes to purchase Keam's collection for ten thousand dollars. The purchase was consummated on Fewkes's return to the reservation in April of 1892. The forty-five hundred ethnological specimens, including baskets, textiles, and ceremonial objects, of which twenty-four hundred were prehistoric to contemporary pots, became known as the Thomas V. Keam Collection of Material Culture. From Hopi, the collection was shipped directly to the Colombian Historical Exposition in Madrid. Fewkes traveled with the collection and directed its installation in one large hall devoted to the Hopi pueblos.

During Fewkes's absence from First Mesa in the winter of 1892–93, Stephen recorded details of the annual Powamu ceremony, a complex ritual for the exorcism of winter and the prognostication of the coming year's crops. Preparations for the ceremony begin at the full moon in January, when the Kachina clan chief plants beans in containers in the kivas, their growth being an omen for the coming season. During the days and nights before the new moon appears and the ceremony begins, the kivas are active with men making prayersticks, singing, telling stories, and repairing kachina masks. The women take part in grinding parties, dances, games, and the preparation of food.

When the new moon is sighted, nine days of ceremony begin. The kachinas have returned to the mesas after having departed the previous July, and they emerge from the kivas to take their parts in the ritual.

Fewkes incorporated Stephen's notes taken during his absence into a report published under his own name,[13] with a footnote that he had worked from Stephen's notes. He described the blessing of kivas and houses by the kachina Ahül, the rubbing of meal against the outer wall next to each door, the kachina's inclinations toward the sun, and his incantations. "He [Ahül] then went to the house of Nampiyo's mother where the same ceremony was performed and so on to the houses of each man or woman of the pueblo who owns a tiponi [a symbolic object of power and origin of a clan] or other principal fetich [sic]."[14] Insignificant as it appears, the reference was Fewkes's first mention of Nampeyo in his published reports and reflects Stephen's recognition of the potter, not his own.

Nampeyo's son, probably William, was initiated during the ceremony in Hano that winter.[15] The eight- to ten-year-old child would have been taken by Nampeyo and Lesso to the plaza, where his waiting godfather handed him an ear of corn. The godfather then led the boy to Tüñwüb, a black-masked kachina with black beard, stomping in place, yucca whips in his hands. Instructing the boy to cast a handful of meal toward the kachina, the godfather undressed William, turned him around with his back to the kachina, "who has all this time maintained his trotting motion but without advancing. Tüñwüb then plies one of his whips vigorously, giving the boy five or six forcible lashes on the back, and the godfather withdraws the screaming boy and ties one of the prayer-feath-

7. "Potter at work, Hano." James Mooney, 1893. (Smithsonian Institution Photo #1875–B–1).

These previously unidentified photos of Nampeyo and her mother, White Corn, were taken by Mooney of the Bureau of Ethnology. Life-size figures of kachinas and villagers were modeled from his photographs for dioramas for the ethnological exhibit in the Field Columbian Exposition in Chicago in 1893. (Two of four photographs of Nampeyo and White Corn)

8. "Potters coiling & polishing, Hano." James Mooney, 1893. (Smithsonian Institution Photo #1875–A–1)

ers he has prepared upon the boy's scalp."[16] Nampeyo, standing nearby, watching and waiting, would have quickly covered William and taken him home, being careful to see that he still held his ear of corn.

For four days, William would not have been permitted to eat either salt or flesh, and according to tradition, each morning he would have been taken to a shrine to deposit a prayer-feather and to cast meal to the sun. On the fourth day, just before sunset, William and other young initiates descended the ladder into the kiva where, for the first time, they looked upon unmasked kachinas and learned that the spirits were portrayed by men of the family and village.

During the last days of the ceremony, then as now, gifts are given to the children by the kachinas, and bean plants sprouted in the kivas are added to stews for the final feast. For people on the mesa, winter is long. From the full moon of Powamu and the planting of beans to the last feast, five weeks of prayers and rituals serve to exorcise the cold, to help warm the earth, and to ensure a bountiful harvest the following year.

James Mooney of the Bureau of Ethnology arrived on the mesa in January of 1893 during the Powamu ceremony. His purpose was to take photographs and make a Hopi collection for the ethnological exhibit to be held at the Field Columbian Exposition in Chicago. During his month-long stay, he photographed kachinas and villagers so that life-sized figures could be prepared for the exhibition to represent the domestic life and ceremonies of the people.

Among these photographs is one of an unidentified potter at work in Hano and three more photos of two potters; Mooney had photographed Nampeyo and her mother, White Corn. In the photograph of her alone, Nampeyo holds a bowl, and another painted bowl is on the ground at her feet. Both bowls appear to have slightly incurved rims, curvilinear designs within, and bold frets on the exteriors. In the photos taken with her mother, Nampeyo is coiling a small jar while White Corn holds a bowl. Several bowls, canteens, and small mounds of clay surround them. The photographs confirm Nampeyo's competence as an expert potter as early as 1893.

Fewkes returned to the mesa to continue his studies that summer and to observe the August Snake Dance in Walpi, but he left before an influenza epidemic swept through the villages during the winter. Nampeyo and women of every household, no doubt, tried to protect their families from the outbreak by "smoking the house":[17] burning juniper in a small vessel and carrying the pungent, smoking charcoal one, two, three, four times around the perimeter of each room.

Many fell ill despite the customary precaution, including Stephen, who seemed unable to regain his health. A shaman from the middle village asked Stephen's permission to try to find the cause of his illness. After receiving payment of a few yards of calico, he took some quartz and pebbles from a pouch and prayed: "Steve, our friend, lies here ill and speechless, maybe you will show me what the ill is, maybe you will show me what has cut off his voice."[18] Taking one of the crystals between finger and thumb, he placed it close to his eye and looked through it at Stephen; then he held it at arm's length and bent forward to look through it again. He swayed back and forth in this manner in silence for several minutes before pressing the crystal against Stephen's right breast, a point where Stephen had experienced severe pain. The shaman scored the spot with a pale-green stone knife, enough to draw blood, and placed his mouth on the wound. After exhaling and inhaling against the wound several times, he withdrew into his mouth "an abominable looking, arrow shaped, headless sort of a centipede"[19] that he spat into Stephen's hand. Instantly, the shaman carried the insect to the cliff's edge to exorcise it. Returning to Stephen, he instructed him to drink a special herb water for the following four days.

Despite the shaman's ministrations, Stephen's illness continued into spring, when he sent a message to Keam asking for help. Finding his friend so weak that he could not stand, Keam took Stephen to his house to care for him. In April of 1894 Stephen died, presumably of tuberculosis. Keam buried his friend in a grave on the edge of a wash in the hills near the trading post, exposed to the relentless sun and seen only from the trader's house on the knoll. Keam ringed the grave with rocks and placed a sandstone cross at Stephen's head that reads:

> In memory of
> A. M. STEPHEN
> WHO DEPARTED THIS LIFE
> Apr. 18, 1894   Aged 49 years
> his life devoted to science and good deeds

One month earlier in Boston another life had ended, the life of one also attracted to the Hopis, whom she had never seen. Mrs. Hemenway died before the museum she envisioned for the Keam Collection was built. Her heirs and trustees decided to abandon her project, choosing the Peabody Museum at Harvard University as depository for the collection. Fewkes agreed to supervise an exhibit of a representative group of the artifacts at the museum. In January of 1895 he wrote to his friend Frederick Webb Hodge of the Bureau of American Ethnology (its name having been changed the previous year from the Bureau of Ethnology) that he expected to complete his work for the Hemenway Expedition. Funding had stopped with the death of his patroness, and he expressed the hope that he could secure other support for his anthropological research. That year upon recommendation by Hodge, Fewkes received an appointment to work for the bureau itself.

While Keam eulogized his friend in the solitude of barren hills, Fewkes, newly appointed to the exclusive ranks of the bureau, began to discredit Stephen's pioneering role in anthropology. Fewkes had valued Stephen's objectivity, meticulous attention to detail, and integrity, and he had incorporated his observations of Hopi life and culture into his own reports while Stephen was alive. After Stephen's death, however, Fewkes denigrated his source as "that enthusiastic student, the late A. M. Stephen."[20]

Thomas Keam had made his collection of ancient Hopi artifacts over many years, led by Tom Polacca on forays to the many ruins known to him. Stephen had enthusiastically joined in the search, cataloging each piece by description, condition, analysis of design, related mythological legend, and use of the vessel. In doing so, Stephen had undertaken the first typology of prehistoric Southwestern ceramics. After Stephen's death, Fewkes condemned Stephen's catalog of the collection as unworthy of publication and turned his attention to his own appointment within the bureau. Interest in the collection waned, effectively relegating the Thomas V. Keam Collection of Material Culture to storage rooms of the Peabody Museum for half a century. In 1943, the director of the museum began to accession and catalog the items but lacked the funds for research and analysis. Not until 1975 did the collection receive scholarly scrutiny and recognition of its historic importance.[21]

Sikyatki and the Snake Dance

"Our landlady makes the best pottery in town."
— *McNitt*, Richard Wetherill: Anasazi

Despite the intrusion of increasing numbers of visitors, the physical condition of the mesa remained unchanged. Debris piled upon debris, empty rooms filled with discarded ceremonial objects and pottery sherds, new floors covered old trash. Excrement lay where it fell, jars of urine for dying yarns stood outside doors, and dung used for firing pottery dried in storage rooms adding pungency to the houses. Countless burros, dogs, pigs, and turkeys added their wastes. Fastidious visitors unprepared for the native ambience experienced shock. The lingering impression was described in the Extra Census Bulletin of the 1890 federal census: "Moqui pueblos are now generally a mass of filth and dirt, the accumulation of ages."[1]

In an effort to move the people off the mesa, the government began to build simple stone houses with red iron roofs at the foot of the trail. Secure in their clan dwellings on the mesas, the people saw no reason to occupy individual family houses below. Using them instead for intermittent income, Nampeyo and other women who owned them rented the houses to artists who visited the mesas, painters and photographers who empathized with their people. As the little settlement of unoccupied houses grew, outsiders identified it informally by its first inhabitant, Capitan Tom, and it became known as Polacca.

During a heavy rainstorm at the end of July 1895, a group traveling in buckboards arrived among the randomly built government houses in Polacca and made camp in a peach orchard near the spring. Jesse Walter Fewkes had returned on his initial assignment for the Bureau of American Ethnology. The former zoologist who had worked as an ethnologist under the sponsorship of Mrs. Hemenway had been sent into the field by the bureau in the role of archaeologist. His instructions were to make as large a collection as possible of objects pertaining to pueblo life in the cliff houses of the Southwest.

After uncovering disappointingly few objects in the valley of the Rio Verde, Fewkes abandoned his focus on cliff dwellings and moved northeast to Antelope Mesa, where a change in prehistoric Hopi pottery had occurred nearly six centuries earlier. About 1300, women in the region began to shape vessels with clay that fired yellow, a departure from the more common gray or white vessels of that time. In the pueblo of Awatovi, potters painted their jars and bowls before firing with symmetrical, geometric designs in black, and in Jeddito, with freer, often asymmetrical black designs.

Fewkes hired a Hopi crew as laborers to excavate for pottery in the ruins of Awatovi, but the hard ground made extracting whole pots nearly impossible. The eventual defection of the crew to their mesa homes compelled Fewkes to move on to Polacca, where he was joined by his friend from the bureau, Frederick Webb Hodge. Rain temporarily postponed their intended plans to excavate Sikyatki. The pueblo had been abandoned or destroyed before Spaniards explored the area in the sixteenth century, but ceramics made by its residents lay concealed by the drifting sands and buried with the dead. Contemporary with or following shortly after the black-on-yellow style change on Antelope Mesa, Sikyatki Polychrome vessels were painted with black designs enhanced with red on yellow clay. Skilled potters shaped graceful jars of spacious diameter, often flattened to low silhouettes and painted with sweeping curves, stylized birds, animals, and floral representations.

While they waited for the storm to abate, Fewkes and Hodge spent their time on the mesa, listening to old ones tell legends and watching priests in the kivas make prayer plumes and repaint kachina masks. On July 24 they were able to explore the ruins of Sikyatki, which Hodge described in his field journal as "an extensive ruin of stone. . . . The ground is covered with sherds of the finest pottery both in texture and decoration that I have seen."[2] On July 26, the group broke camp in Polacca and moved around the base of the mesa to the site of that ancient pueblo.

In addition to F.W. Hodge, Fewkes's work party consisted of James S. Judd, photographer Erwin Baer, and the cook and driver, S. Goddard. Others in the group included the second Mrs. Fewkes, Mrs. Hodge, who made accurate, colored drawings of the excavated vessels,[3] and a visiting student, G.P. Winship. From the time of his arrival in Polacca, Hodge kept a personal journal in which he described the residents he encountered and the daily activities at the site. After his return to Washington, Fewkes wrote two lengthy official reports, a preliminary report for the Smithsonian Institution[4] and another for the Bureau of American Ethnology;[5] they differed from Hodge's field notes on several points.

Fewkes wrote that his crew consisted of fifteen Hopi workmen.[6] Hodge had recorded ten workmen, three each assigned to the supervision of Hodge, Judd, and Baer, and one who served as assistant to the cook, Goddard.[7] Fewkes reported that there was no evidence that Sikyatki had been destroyed by fire,[8] while Hodge recorded that the ancient village showed signs of destruction by fire because charred remains of thatched roofing, corn cobs, small beams, and other items were seen in nearly all the rooms excavated.[9]

Fewkes reported that Indians from neighboring villages visited the site, and both Fewkes and Hodge told of being admonished by old men who scattered piki over unearthed bones and skeletons as an offering to Masauwûh, the death god. Excavation progressed slowly, exacerbated by a general strike of the workers when one was admonished for taking beads from a grave. An understanding was reached between Fewkes and the laborers, who agreed to stay overnight and return to work the following morning. Toward the end of the excavation, it was necessary to offer prizes to the Hopi crew: overalls to the worker finding the most pottery, fifty cents for an unbroken vessel, and a smaller sum for a damaged one. After two and a half weeks of excavating, the crew packed the un-earthed vessels for shipment to the National Museum. They formed a collection of coiled and indented ware, smooth un-decorated pots, and yellow vessels painted with red, black, and white designs that remain among the most exquisite ceramics produced by any culture.[10]

To the villagers on First Mesa, however, the activities at Sikyatki were not of primary importance, for the nine-day ritual of the Snake ceremony in Walpi had already begun before Fewkes had completed his excavation of the barren ruin. Clansmen had gathered snakes for the ceremony from the four directions: northwest, southwest, southeast, and northeast. Men were participating in kiva activities, making and depositing prayer sticks, and conducting initiation of members into the Snake Society. Women were making quantities of blue piki and preparing ceremonial food for male participants and visitors. On the ninth day, during the concluding dance on the plaza to which so many visitors had been attracted, painted dancers held the snakes in their mouths before releasing them and carrying them back to their natural habitats. The Snake ceremony's importance to the mesa people is a petition to the spirits for rain.

Less than accurate reports of the ceremony had found their way into print, the first in 1879.[11] A highly embellished secondhand account published in 1882 stated, "At some dances dogs are killed and savagely devowered [sic] by the actors who seem to relish the flesh ere it has ceased to quiver."[12] More objective was the report by Lt. John G. Bourke, who spent most of his military career recording customs of Indians and collecting their crafts. Having heard unconfirmed rumors of "peculiar ceremonies to be noticed among the Moquis,"[13] he set out with artist Peter Moran from Santa Fe in August of 1881 on the new railroad heading west into Arizona. His diary describing his adventures en route, the ceremony and his reaction to it, and his account of the people and their culture was edited into a volume for popular reading and published in 1884.[14] Each odd-numbered year as crowds of visitors increased, professional photographers clamored for the most advantageous place to set up the tripods for their glass-plate view cameras, while journalists and ethnologists scribbled rapidly in their notebooks.

Among many drawn to the ceremony in 1895, Richard Wetherill, an indefatigable explorer of Anasazi sites in the Four Corners area, climbed the trail to First Mesa accompanied by his brother Clayton and several friends. In a conversation conducted partly in Navajo and partly in English and supplemented by many gestures, Wetherill asked an old man where they might stay. Motioning them to follow, the villager led them back to the house at the top of the trail where, after knocking on the door, he left them. The knock brought the immediate response of "a short middle-aged man and his plump, smiling wife."[15] Lesso beckoned them inside, but the presence of several children in the crowded room made them reluctant to join the family. When they indicated that they would prefer to sleep outdoors, they were offered a terrace on the rooftop where they laid out their bedrolls.

It is frequently difficult to know whether writers were referring to the Corn clan house or to the Tobacco clan house. When Tom Polacca married Okong, he would have slept at her house and furnished food and wood for the family, but according to custom, he would have entertained in his Corn clan house. When second- and third-floor rooms were added to the two clan houses, the terraces probably intermingled because the two structures were adjacent, the Tobacco clan facing the plaza and the Corn clan facing east at the top of the trail. Adding further confusion, Polacca had built a house near the spring at the base of the mesa. With good reason we can assume that he entertained government officials in his house below, lived with his wife and children in the Tobacco clan dwellings a major part of the time, and entertained unofficial visitors in the Corn clan dwellings of White Corn and Nampeyo.

Referring to the Corn clan house at the top of the trail, one of Wetherill's friends noted in his journal that they "stayed at the house of a certain Tom Polyke [Polacca] who is known as one of the most progressive Moquis. He is one who favors schools and such modern institutions. Our landlady makes the best pottery in town or in fact in any of the towns so far as I know."[16] During their visit, several pieces of the "landlady's" pottery were added to their collection of kachinas and woven goods, stashed under a tarpaulin next to Nampeyo's house.

One night, after they had retired to the terrace, Wetherill and his friends heard a commotion of shouts and commands, as if the village were under attack. Residents ran from their houses and gathered at the edge of the mesa outside Nampeyo's house, trying to see the cause of the clamor in the darkness below.

Amateur photographer Adam Clark Vroman and three friends had arrived at the base of the mesa, where they faced a dilemma they had not anticipated. One of the group was a newspaper writer, a Mrs. Lowe, an obese woman of about 250 pounds encased in a long black dress. A wide-brimmed black hat framed her full face, and she waved a large fan to ease her discomfort in the hot night. The problem was how to get Mrs. Lowe to the top of the mesa, for she surely would be unable to climb the rocky path.

Cries of alarm from Mrs. Lowe interspersed with shouted directions from the three men had been heard by Wetherill, his friends, and the astonished villagers before they could see the strange procession ascending the trail. Struggling to keep their footing, sixteen Hopi men shouldered a pole ladder held horizontally with Mrs. Lowe balanced precariously aloft. Vroman followed, carrying fifty pounds of cameras, tripods, glass negatives, and other photographic gear, and behind him, the two other baggage-laden men brought up the rear. When they reached the top, Mrs. Lowe was lowered to the ground in front of the Corn clan dwellings, and with all of their impedimenta, the group made their way through the plaza of a thoroughly awakened Hano to a house in the middle village, where they settled in for their stay.

Many others converged on the mesa to observe the Snake ritual: ranchers, traders, government representatives, Navajos in colorful dress, and distant Hopi family and clan members from other pueblos. By the time Vroman had set up his tripod in the Walpi plaza for the final dance, a dozen other photographers were already in position. His excavation at

Sikyatki completed, Fewkes, who had witnessed the ceremony in 1891 and 1893, ascended the trail to join the crowd gathered around the plaza. As the dance ended, the painted dancers dropped the snakes onto a circle of cornmeal, plunged their arms into the wriggling mass, grasped snakes indiscriminately, and ran down the cliff to return them to the desert below.

The stunned spectators dispersed to explore the mesa and to buy souvenirs displayed on rugs outside the houses: baskets, kachina dolls, pottery, and trinkets. Knowledgeable visitors stopped at Nampeyo's house to purchase what had become known as the finest pottery on the mesa.

> Her money that she make she put into a pot that she had smoked. You put food into the pot—juniper—that's food for the pot. Then you burn it. Smoke is medicine, it makes the pot black inside. Then you talk to it and it makes a perfect pot to keep things safe. (1988)

Fewkes joined the crowd, passing through the middle village of Sichomovi and the plaza of Hano, past Nampeyo's house and down the trail. He and his companions broke camp, and he returned to Washington. Far from the barren excavation site and the crowded, colorful spectacle of the Snake Dance, Fewkes wrote a preliminary account of his expedition for the Smithsonian Institution that included the following comments:

> Even the Indians from the neighboring villages who visited me and saw the beautiful ware which I exhumed from these desolate mounds and sands did not fail to contrast the past with the present. The best potter of East Mesa, an intelligent woman from Hano named Nampio, acknowledged that her productions were far inferior to those of the women of Sikyatki and she begged permission to copy some of the decorations for future inspiration. The sight of this dusky woman and her husband copying designs of ancient ware and acknowledging their superiority was instructive in many ways.[17]

By the time that Fewkes wrote his lengthy final report for the Bureau of American Ethnology, he was alleging that, since his excavations at Sikyatki, Hopi potters were disposing "as

Sikyatki ware, to unsuspecting white visitors, some of their modern objects of pottery. These fraudulent pieces are often very cleverly made."[18] More specifically of Nampeyo he wrote:

> The most expert modern potter at East Mesa is Nampéo, a Tanoan woman who is a thorough artist in her line of work. Finding a better market for ancient than for modern ware, she cleverly copies old decorations, and imitates the Sikyatki ware almost perfectly. She knows where the Sikyatki potters obtained their clay, and uses it in her work. Almost any Hopi who has a bowl to sell will say that it is ancient, and care must always be exercised in accepting such claims.[19]

In the final report, Fewkes did not place Nampeyo at the excavation site begging permission to copy designs nor did Hodge's field notes. Hodge's journal reflected his interest in the people he observed, including storytellers, kiva workers, Tom "Polakaka," girls singing while grinding corn, Navajos, a worker who surreptitiously took beads from a grave, elders who scattered piki over bones, and the Hopi crew, seven of whom he named. Hodge made no note describing the best potter of Hano and her husband copying designs from the ancient ware at the site.

Curious potters must have visited the excavation in spite of their preparations for the Snake Dance, and Nampeyo was probably among them. Women were familiar with individual prehistoric vessels, but the extravagant display as each was wiped clean of its sandy burial would have added to the vocabulary of forms and designs already known to them.

Fewkes's conflicting statements about Nampeyo indicate that he was aware of her stature as an expert potter at the time of his excavation, but they demonstrate his personal need to subvert her work to his own archaeological discovery. Contrary to his reports, the excavation of Sikyatki in 1895 was not the stimulus for a new pottery style. It served to energize a revival already begun.

Missionaries

"Immortal souls to be saved."
   —*Wright,* Hopi Material Culture

In the summer of 1896, Jesse Walter Fewkes returned to the Moqui Reservation with Walter Hough of the National Museum to excavate old Shongopovi at the base of Second Mesa.[1] Fragments of pottery littered the ruin, and excavation of the cemetery yielded over a hundred fine specimens. Fewkes reported that they were "the finest old Tusayan ware, cream and red being the predominating colors, while fragments of coiled black and white ware are likewise common."[2]

The two archaeologists moved camp to Polacca in time for Fewkes to attend the Flute ceremony at Walpi. Having learned of the pottery Fewkes had excavated from the ruins of old Shongopovi, Nampeyo visited his camp to copy designs.[3] Hough asked the potter if he could watch her work, so at a prearranged time he climbed the trail and entered the cool stone house with its "curious belongings hung on the wall or thrust above the great ceiling beams."[4] He found the old couple, White Corn and Quootsva, sitting in the room along with Lesso, who was spinning wool. A baby, probably Nellie, was secured in her cradleboard for an afternoon nap.

Nampeyo made her entrance down a ladder from a second-story room. A pair of bare feet were followed by the short manta-clad figure smiling a greeting as she emerged into the room. Patient and gracious as she was to all visitors, Nampeyo demonstrated her skill for Hough, who took detailed notes as she shaped the clay and rapidly covered three small vessels with designs.

Deeply impressed, Hough praised Nampeyo as a remarkable woman, an artist whose taste and skill would continue to mature. "Everyone who visits Tusayan will bring away as a souvenir some of the work of Nampeo, the potter who lives with her husband Lesu in the house of her parents in Hano, the little Tewa village on the great Walpi mesa near the gap."[5] Hough returned to Washington with seven of her bowls for the collection of the National Museum (Plate 1). The bowls— $7^1/_4$ to $8^3/_4$ inches in diameter with interior designs of stylistic kachina faces, figures, and abstract curvilinear designs—are the earliest documented examples of Nampeyo's work.[6]

The following year, in August of 1897, nearly two hundred spectators congregated around the plaza in Walpi, attracted by descriptive articles and dramatic photographs of the Snake Dance. Among the visitors were George H. Pepper, director of excavation in Chaco Canyon; A. C. Vroman, with his camera and equipment; George Wharton James, a writer of colorful but shallow travelogues; and Frederick Monsen, writer, photographer, and crusader for Indian rights. After the visitors had left and quiet routine had resumed, Fewkes determined to remain until April to record all the winter rituals. During his stay, many Hopis and Tewas made their annual pilgrimage to Zuni for the Shalako ceremony,[7] unaware that smallpox had ravaged the pueblo. Upon their return, the epidemic spread throughout the villages on First and Second mesas. Corpses were thrown outside houses with no one to bury them. The superintendent of the Moqui Training School in Keams Canyon immediately quarantined all the children, who were not permitted to return home for a full year. "When we did come home, a lot of people we knew on First Mesa and Second Mesa were missing. Almost every family had lost somebody."[8] Nampeyo's old father, Quootsva, may have perished in the epidemic, for he was no longer living when the 1900 federal census was taken.

The Indian agent called for a division from Fort Wingate to perform the grisly task of disposing of the dead. The bodies were thrown into crevices, covered with oil, and then burned in mass cremations. Alarmed by the contagious outbreak, Fewkes fled to the railroad. He expressed disappointment and fright in a letter to his friend Hodge, along with the hope that he would live.[9]

Fewkes himself became the protagonist of a legend after he departed that winter. He had been in a kiva taking notes during part of the Wuwuchim ceremony when the elders warned him to leave, to go home, and to lock his door. Masauwûh, the terrifying death god who carries a flaming torch, was coming. Fewkes complied. That night while he was working on his notes, according to the legend, a tall man appeared next to him. Surprised, Fewkes asked, "What do you want and how did you get in here?" The man replied, "I have come to entertain you." Fewkes offered him a cigarette that the stranger lit with a stream of fire from his mouth. Realizing that his visitor was the dreaded god, Fewkes proclaimed his belief in Masauwûh, who then cast a spell on him. The Hopis say that Fewkes related his experience to priests in the kiva the next day. "And it was not long after that Dr. Fewkes went away but it was not on account of the smallpox as you now know."[10]

Fewkes made his last extended visit to the reservation during the winter of 1899, but he continued intermittently during the remaining years of his career to publish material gathered during the decade of the 1890s.

Anthropologists had been drawn to the Hopi mesas to study a culture that was structured by tradition and ceremony, by clan and by gender. The alienness that attracted anthropologists, however, was anathema to Christian ideology, and various denominations determined to transform the mesa people into acceptable images of white men and to convert them to Christianity.

Franciscan friars had arrived in Awatovi as early as 1692 to build missions and establish Catholicism. The blue-robed priests brought sheep and cattle, peach trees, and tools to replace the handmade implements used in the fields and homes. But labor enforced upon the natives, condemnation of kachinas, and suppression of ceremonies provoked a purge of Catholicism seventy years later, when Hopis from other mesas attacked Awatovi around 1700 and destroyed it.

One hundred and fifty years of relative isolation allowed

the people to celebrate life without intrusion. In 1858, the charismatic Jacob Hamblin received instructions from Brigham Young, president of the Church of Jesus Christ of Latter-day Saints, "to take a company of men and visit the Moquis … to learn something of the character and condition of this people, and to take advantage of any opening there might be to preach the gospel to them and to do good."[11] During frequent visits over a period of fifteen years, Young and accompanying missionaries achieved considerable success in conversion, including that of Tom Polacca.

In 1893, the Mission Board of the Mennonite Church asked the Reverend H.R. Voth to establish a mission in the Hopi area. Voth chose the most conservative village, Oraibi, in which to carry out his assignment. He and his wife believed that under the Hopis' "outward filth and degradation there were splendid lovable natures, immortal souls to be saved,"[12] so they learned the language and proselytized in the streets. Like Stephen, Voth became a passionate ethnologist without formal training in the field. And like Fewkes, he became a controversial figure in Hopi history.

Voth pushed the tolerance of Oraibi elders with his aggression, forcing his way into kivas to study ceremonies. Though he failed to convert residents of the old pueblos, he attracted the attention of George Dorsey of the Field Columbian Museum of Chicago, which published his definitive monographs, and the Fred Harvey Company, which used him as a consultant.

Voth must have been aware of Nampeyo on First Mesa, though contemporary pottery was not his primary interest and no reference to the potter is found in his writings. The erroneous report that Voth and George Dorsey sponsored Nampeyo's attendance at a Santa Fe Railway Exhibition in Chicago in 1898 originated after Nampeyo's death.[13]

In the late 1890s, the Baptist Church assigned missionaries to the mesas. Field matron Sarah Abbott and two young female acolytes settled into Polacca and, with the zeal of evangelists, frequently climbed the trail to the plazas of the three villages on First Mesa where they held "street meetings." They would sing a few hymns accompanied by guitar, read selections from the Bible, and give short discourses on the Right Way, assisted by a Hopi interpreter. While they sermonized, burros brayed, dogs barked, and children laughed and ran about. When the young women asked entrance to homes, wives went on singing at their chores and husbands expressed anger at the intrusion.

Those young Baptist missionaries regarded Hopi ceremonies with abhorrence and felt that Satan was at work. They were as repulsed as they were eager to save souls. Regardless of their beliefs, they did attempt to improve the physical conditions and health of the villagers. They built a laundry where the women could wash clothes, taught them to sew clothing that was lighter than their black homespun wool garments, and cared for the sick, assisting when necessary in the hospital at Keams Canyon. They were eager to help and to listen.

With righteous enthusiasm, they bombarded the superintendent in residence with requests and suggestions, including the need for brooms and the help of school children to sweep all villages in order to clean them. Then-superintendent Lemmon responded that the thought of intelligent white women sweeping the villages was as repugnant as a filthy village itself.

Early conversions were few, but they became more numerous after 1918 when missionaries were each given a specific number of non-Christians to whom they personally carried the gospel every week. "One thing is clear. The Hopis and Tewas who convert from traditional religion have taken themselves out of our traditional ways. The missionaries have had a great deal to do with the destruction of Hopi-Tewa religion.… I guess you can't blame the missionaries too much. They are doing what they believe they are supposed to do. If our traditional religion is passing, you have to blame the Hopis and Tewas themselves."[14]

While passive residents tolerated the presumptuous interference, others turned hostile, retaliating against those among their own who did not decry change. The progressive Tom Polacca became an obvious target of their anger.

With a passion for life, Polacca had fulfilled many roles: leader, interpreter, policeman, and vocal advocate for education. His conversion to Mormonism as a young man was severely tested when he received only sporadic support from visiting Latter-day Saints missionaries. As one recent missionary to Hopi explains, "It isn't easy for Indians to form the intense, affectionate relationship that you have with missionaries, and then have them say it is over for now. It's too hard on them."[15] But Polacca instructed his children to join no other church. "The brothers will come again and you will know them because they will call you brother and sister. . . . You will know them because they have our book, the Book of Mormon."[16]

Conservative Hopis openly criticized Polacca's progressive activities and his religious prophecies that the last days were at hand, that it was time for them to move down from the mesa top. When something went wrong, the Hopis complained, "Well, you can thank Tom Polacca for that."[17] As the antagonism grew, Polacca fortified his house near the spring against hostile villagers from the mesa who, on many nights, gathered outside threatening to kill him.[18] Fearing for his life and for his family, he moved with Okong and his children to the stone shelters on the ranch, abandoning his house at the base of the trail.

The frequently repeated statement that Tom Polacca operated a store around which the village of Polacca grew has no validity.

> He goes around far away to buy things, look for things,
> cows, cattle, sheep, buckskin, but he never had any store.[19]
> (1986)

The error may have been caused by confusion between the two Toms: Tom Polacca and Tom Pavatea, who opened a trading post in Polacca in 1896. Orphaned as a child, Pavatea had been raised by a Tewa woman before being forcibly carried off to school from which he repeatedly ran away. He had worked for Thomas Keam herding sheep and had married Willie Healing's sister, Quang, of the Tobacco clan, before opening the store that served the mesa residents. Pavatea was a large, benevolent man, generous with his own people, gracious to visitors, trusted by dealers outside the reservation.

Inside his stone post, he stocked staples for the residents and the crafts that he took in exchange. Behind the building were corrals that held bartered livestock that would be sent to Keam for transport outside the reservation.

Pavatea possessed all the attributes of a successful trader. Polacca had neither the time from his many activities to operate a store nor the confidence of his people to patronize it. When he allowed the Baptist field matron to convert his abandoned house at the base of the trail into a missionary house, he was shunned by his own people.

Tolerant of all, Pavatea befriended the missionaries and listened to their story, but to their regret, he never followed "The Way." "I have not the time. I have not the money. Too many of my people need food and clothes. Too many must be cared for. I am too busy to be a Christian!"[20]

Making a Pot

"Others were jealous." (1990)

Baptist field matron Sarah Abbott took the federal census on the Moqui Reservation in 1900 and recorded, in an unidentified residence, Tom Polacca and his wife, Okong; their sons Howelah, Nelson, Clyde, and Stanley; a daughter, Kahee, and infant son Vinton.

Living in the Corn clan house in Hano were the elderly White Corn, Nampeyo and Lesso, and their two young children: Nellie, born about 1896, and infant son Wesley, born in 1899. Annie, not yet twenty years old and her husband, Willie Healing, lived in the household, as did two of Nampeyo's Corn clan brothers, Kano and Squash. Not recorded in the census was Nampeyo's last child, Fannie, born late in 1900. Several months later in 1901, Annie bore Nampeyo's first grandchild, Rachel.

Family members in the crowded household were as vulnerable to diseases and contagious ailments as other residents on the mesas. The increasing number of visitors, unsanitary conditions, and the lack of medical treatment were responsible for epidemics of smallpox, influenza, tuberculosis, dysentery, and trachoma, a chronic conjunctivitis.

Dr. Joshua Miller, who moved to Arizona in 1883 to practice medicine, became an avid collector of native artifacts and, subsequently, became concerned about the welfare of the Hopi people. He voluntarily ministered to them during summer months and frequently received gifts of crafts in return for his care. At an unknown date between 1890 and Miller's death in 1901, the doctor treated Nampeyo's eyes, presumably for the early stages of trachoma, and received a large canteen with kachina design (Plate 2) from her in exchange.

Trachoma is an insidious eye disease that alternately goes into remission and recurs to produce granulation, scarring, and eventual opacity of the cornea. If untreated with antibiotics, it can produce extensive loss of vision after a period of about twenty years. Before the availability of such medication, Indian traders on the reservation treated the prevalent infection among residents with Argyrol, an antiseptic solution that temporarily checked the progress of the disease but did not cure it.

Nampeyo's pre-1901 gift to Dr. Miller is the first documented indication of the disease that eventually impaired her sight. It occurred at a time when Nampeyo was about to begin a decade of unparalleled artistic achievement. Within a few years, travel brochures and booklets describing the Southwest featured at least one picture of Nampeyo and her pottery. When visitors found her in person at the top of the trail, they photographed her, purchased a souvenir, and frequently requested a demonstration of her skill. Nampeyo would graciously comply.

The following composite description was taken from accounts by Walter Hough (*The Hopi Indians*), Samuel Barrett ("Pottery,"), and Alexander Stephen (*Hopi Journal of Alexander Stephen*), from comments by descendants of Nampeyo, and from other observers.

Nampeyo dug her clay from several sources both on and near the mesa and carried it on her back to the house to refine, coil, and to shape. The dry clay would be pulverized on a large rock, placed in a container with water to soften it, and mixed to a wet paste. Then:

She put her feet in there to get out all the pebbles. They squeeze out between her toes and she throws them away. (1982)

Alexander Stephen reported that the women's feet were used "in this kneading process with considerable mobility."[1]

The paste was transferred to a flat stone, an old kneading stone found in a ruin, upon which Nampeyo kneaded the clay to a smooth consistency with her hands, removing any remaining foreign matter that might later cause the vessel to break in drying or in firing. Two pieces of sandstone were then rubbed together to produce a fine sand that was added to the rich clay as a temper, rendering it harder and less likely to break. If the clay felt too wet, it was daubed on a board and set in the sun to dry to the proper consistency. If it had become too dry, a little water was added.

> You have to pound it like that with your hand to break all the bubbles out, and you have to work it with your hand again and pound it until it all sticks together solid. (1982)

Leaving the mass on the stone, Nampeyo would break off a small piece of clay, and working it with her thumbs, shape a bottom for the pot, which she placed in a dish or pan, a puki. Breaking off subsequent pieces, she rolled each between her palms to make a long coil. The first was placed on the edge of the formed bottom and pressed and smoothed between thumb and fingers to make it adhere. The next coil was added to the preceding one, each being pressed and smoothed. Keeping her hands damp so that the clay would not dry out, Nampeyo worked quickly, and the ropes of clay rolled from her palms "in a marvelous way, and . . . excited a smile from the family sitting around as interested spectators."[2]

As the shape grew out and up with each added coil, a gourd or squash rind was used to smooth the pot, inside and out. When Nampeyo felt the shape would support no more wet clay, she would set it aside to dry until more coils could be added. This step might be repeated several times until she had finished shaping the vessel. Then, the final coil would be added to the orifice, the opening shaped, and the pot set aside to dry thoroughly.

The rough, dry pot was dressed with a fine sandstone smoother that left grainy striae on the surface.

> My grandmother used long strokes, not little short ones like others, back and forth this way. Sometimes you can tell. (1988)

9. "Nampeyo coiling a clay jar." Adam Clark Vroman, 1901. (Smithsonian Institution Photo #32357–F)

The coil of wet clay that Nampeyo is adding to the unfinished vessel will be smoothed with her fingers to adhere and more coils will be added until the vessel attains the shape she visualizes. (One of several photos taken by Vroman of Nampeyo at work)

Nampeyo frequently applied a thin slip of white clay to the surface with a swab of wool, and the pot was set aside again to dry. The final polishing was done with a smooth stone or pebble that was repeatedly dipped into water.

The materials from which Nampeyo's paints were made also had to be gathered from the land. The red, white, and dark brown paints, all mineral colors, were ground on a slab and mixed with water. For black paint, beeweed or mustard plant was boiled down to a thick syrup, then dried on a slab or corn husk. Once dried, a small piece would be dissolved in enough water to achieve the desired consistency and color.

As natural as her clay and paints, Nampeyo's brushes were pieces of yucca, chewed at the end to allow the fibers to separate. Using separate brushes for each color, Nampeyo rapidly covered the vessels with spontaneous designs: fine lines, geometric shapes, and broad sweeping scrolls. To cover large areas, she applied the paint with a swab of wool. Once again, the pot was set aside to dry.

> It's hard to put the design inside a bowl. A red square
> around the neck is harder to paint. You have to get your
> lines straight. We don't measure or draw it first. (1982)

One large or several smaller vessels would have been completed before the firing was begun outside. In Stephen's day, "any spot close to the house [was] chosen,"[3] but in her later years Nampeyo fired at the family's Sand Hill ranch.

In a circular ridge of sand, a bed of dried sheep dung was laid and ignited, and the pots were set nearby to be warmed. Several rocks or a grating were placed on top of the smoldering dung to hold the unfired pots, which were carefully covered with fragments of broken pottery to shield them from the fire.

> When she fired the potteries, she covered them first with a
> lot of broken potteries in big pieces; that's so the manure or
> coal won't touch the pottery. Sometimes my grandma used
> coal. If she don't have enough manure she used coal inside
> [probably as a base], then she piled chunks of sheep ma-
> nure [around and above the pottery] just like a bread oven
> until it made a big hill. There used to be a lot of coal around
> there, soft coal. . . . When it's fired with coal, the pot sounds
> tinny. (1982)

Slabs of dried dung carefully laid to form a dome over the pottery gradually ignited from the smoldering base and were allowed to burn out over several hours.

> When she is firing, she usually wash her hair because she is
> perspiring hot. She used to just put her head in the water,
> squeeze [her hair], and roll it up like that. (1982)

The knot of wet hair above Nampeyo's forehead can be seen in many photographs taken while she fired her pottery.

When the dung had burned out and the firing was completed, the ashes would be raked or brushed off the mound and the pots removed with a stick. Wiped clean with a cloth, the pots were then ready for use or for sale.

Photographer Kate Cory noted in her diary that Nampeyo

10. "Nampeyo building a wall of fuel." Adam Clark Vroman, 1901. (Smithsonian Institution Photo #34188–A)

After coiling, polishing, and painting several clay vessels, Nampeyo placed dried sheep dung in a mound around and over the pottery to fire it. The distinctive knot of wet hair above her forehead helped to cool her during the hot procedure.

placed sheep bones in the fire underneath the pots, which, she said, improved them, though she did not indicate in what way.[4] In the same entry, Cory observed that Nampeyo used a plant near Miss Abbott's (formerly Tom Polacca's) house that has "a red burpor [sic] blossom" that she rubbed on the pot to add a touch of smoothness. "These two ways seem to belong to the Tewas, especially Nampeyo. Tewa thinks sheeps' bones were used 'long time ago.'"[5]

I used to go around on the top of the mesa with her to collect old bones to put in the fire. Bones make a hot fire. (1990)

Stephen had another explanation: "Bones of sheep, cattle or deer are sometimes laid in among the dung cakes, this to make the pottery white in the firing; as the bones turn white in burning, they impart this quality of whiteness to the pottery."[6]

The lengthy process from raw clay to finished pot was never free from disappointment, for breaking, cracking, and spalling (a piece of clay's flaking off because of an air bubble or impurity left in the clay) often occurred, particularly during the firing. When Nampeyo attempted to make an extremely large, globose pot for Samuel Barrett of the Milwaukee Public

11. "Nampeyo and her daughter." Sumner W. Matteson, ca. 1900. (Milwaukee Public Museum Photo #44743)

This photo of Nampeyo and Annie was presumptively dated 1901 and Annie mistakenly identified as Nellie by authors Casagrande and Bourns in *Side Trips, The Photography of Sumner W. Matteson*. Comparing Vroman's photos of 1901 with this one by Matteson, several of Nampeyo's descendants have stated that Annie was much younger when this photo was taken, which would date the photo from the mid- to late-1890s.

Museum in 1911, "though five attempts were made . . . none [were] successful."[7]

She is willing, always, willing. She said that herself. (1982)

The firing of pottery always attracted a bevy of children. Holding dried ears of blue corn, they squatted patiently around the smoking, smoldering mound until the potter raked some of the embers into the sand. Then, one by one, they would hand her the dried ears from which she knocked off the kernels. Dropped into the hot coals to pop, the snack was carefully retrieved and savored.

During the decade of the 1890s, only a few vessels made by Nampeyo were documented: two bowls pictured in James Mooney's photograph of the potter taken in 1893 (Photograph 7); a bowl collection made by Walter Hough in 1896 (Plate 1); and the canteen given to Dr. Joshua Miller at an unknown date (Plate 2). The shape of her jars and the style of designs that she painted on them is unknown.[8]

At the turn of the century, Nampeyo was about forty years old and Annie not yet twenty. Annie had inherited Nampeyo's quiet temperament and had learned to make pottery by watching her mother. As indicated by photographs and reports by observers, the two worked together making pottery to sell. Typical of Hopi and Tewa custom, neither mother nor daughter sought individual recognition but set their unsigned vessels on a rug outside their home for visitors to purchase. The pottery that visitors carried away they attributed to Nampeyo.

Lesso's role in Nampeyo's pottery-making has been unrealistically exaggerated. He was a working farmer who had neither extended periods of time nor, very probably, the adeptness to fashion a vessel of elegance. If he assisted Nampeyo with her pottery, he was never seen or photographed doing so.[9]

Nampeyo did not work with potters outside her immediate family. The singular attention that she received created resentment among her contemporaries, and the great volume and diversity of pottery that she and Annie were producing must have created envy.

> Others were jealous. She used to leave her clay outside the house and one day she knew someone had done something to it. She tasted it and they had mixed salt in the clay.
> (1990)

The decade beginning in 1900 was one of significant recognition for Nampeyo. During the first half of the decade, more photographs were taken and documented collections of her work made than in any other period of her career. In the latter half, she traveled from her mesa home three times to demonstrate her skills.

Photographers and Collectors

"The ware of old Nampeyo and her daughter have gone far and wide."
   —*Dorsey,* Indians of the Southwest

During the latter half of the nineteenth century, the American Indian became a unique commodity to be exhibited to a curious public.[1] Anthropologists wanted to educate, but entrepreneurs clamored to entertain. At world's fairs, wild west shows, and industrial exhibitions, paying observers could safely watch groups from various tribes living in artificial surroundings, supposedly carrying on their native customs.

Because the Hopis were more isolated and less approachable, they first became known to the public through photographs of dramatic scenes of the Snake Dance and of other-worldly kachinas. It was necessary for those with greater interest to travel to Hopi to observe this "most primitive" of Indian tribes performing their daily tasks and traditional ceremonies.

Photographer Edward S. Curtis, an early and frequent visitor to Hopi, shared a concern with his peers about the future of all native peoples. He dedicated his life to making a comprehensive photographic record of all tribes before their cultures became extinct. During a thirty-year period, he took over forty thousand photographs and craved the support of the Bureau of American Ethnology for his massive project. It was denied because he worked independently, his credentials were questioned, and he was criticized for posing his subjects and for "romanticizing" them.

In 1900, Curtis took a dramatic photograph of Nampeyo painting a large globose vessel with another beside her that

12. "Nampeyo decorating pottery." Edward S. Curtis, 1900. (Smithsonian Institution Photo #76–5737)

How many photographs Curtis took of Nampeyo is unknown, but she was a favorite subject. He frequently combed out her traditional hair style before photographing her, which made her look younger and prettier by Anglo standards.

may have been the first photograph to identify the potter by name and her work. Nampeyo became one of his favorite subjects when he returned to photograph on the reservation in 1902, 1904, 1906, 1911, 1912, and 1919. How many photographs he took of her is not known, because his work has never been cataloged. His photographs of Nampeyo justify some criticism of the ethnological inaccuracy that he portrayed, for it is apparent that he combed out her characteristic Tewa hairstyle to make her look younger and prettier by Anglo standards. He left remarkable images of the potter at the beginning of the century, nevertheless.

During the summer of 1901, two separate archaeological teams culminated their work in northern Arizona with a visit to First Mesa. One group was sponsored jointly by the National Museum and Peter Goddard Gates of Pasadena, Cali-

fornia, under the direction of Walter Hough; the second was sponsored by the Field Columbian Museum of Chicago under the leadership of George A. Dorsey. Both groups ascended the mesa in time to join the multitudes for the Snake Dance, and members of both groups were attracted to Nampeyo and Annie. Their documentation of pottery made by mother and daughter that summer was impressive.

After two months of excavating ruins in the vicinity of Holbrook, the Museum-Gates expedition was joined by photographer A. C. Vroman. They proceeded on to Jeddito Wash near Keams Canyon for more excavation and then to First Mesa for the ceremony. Vroman had observed and photographed the ritual on previous visits, but in 1901 he found Nampeyo, her family, and a house filled with pottery to be compelling subjects. He posed the potter on a rug outside her

13. "Nampeyo, potter of Hano, with some of her wares." Adam Clark Vroman, 1901. (The Southwest Museum, Los Angeles. Photo #N.30, 539)

The larger vessels in this photo were made by Nampeyo, but the red-slip bowl that Nampeyo is holding and the similar bowl in the back row right were made by the young Annie. Compare with Plate 4.

14. "Annie Healing."
Adam Clark Vroman,
1901. (The Southwest
Museum, Los Angeles.
Photo #N.20698)
   Vroman posed Annie
with many of the same
vessels as those in Photograph 13 of Nampeyo, but
he added another of
Annie's red-slip bowls in
the foreground far right.

stone house (Photograph 13) surrounded by twenty-two vessels of varying sizes: bowls, medium-size jars, two globose pots of similar shape to those photographed by Curtis in 1900, and four wide-diameter Sikyatki-shape jars. He also posed Annie on the same rug with many of the same vessels, some of them rearranged, a second paint stone added (Photograph 14).

   Why did Vroman photograph each potter separately and in the same manner? Annie in her late teens could not yet have had the capability to coil or to paint many of the expertly crafted vessels in the photographs. Perhaps Vroman was overwhelmed by the quantity of refined pottery he found at Nampeyo's house and, with an artist's whim, photographed Annie as a gesture of friendship to her mother. Or, not being able to differentiate between vessels made by Nampeyo and Annie, perhaps he wanted to document each potter in the uniquely picturesque setting.

Vroman also photographed four Corn clan generations: Nampeyo's mother (White Corn), Nampeyo, and Annie holding her young Rachel on her lap (Photograph 15). His camera recorded Nampeyo inside the house, coiling a pot (Photograph 9) and kneading her clay, and Lesso, cutting mutton (Photograph 4) and fitting newly made moccasins on the photographer himself. The vessels that had been moved to the rug outside for other photographs are shown on shelves and along the banco in the interior pictures. When Vroman left the mesa with all his photographic equipment, he also carried several of the vessels with him for his personal collection.[2]

When the team sponsored by the Field Museum arrived on the mesa, the accompanying photographer, Sumner Matteson, who had photographed Nampeyo and Annie on a previous visit,[3] apparently did not photograph the potter again.

15. "Nampeyo and Family." Adam Clark Vroman, 1901. (The Southwest Museum, Los Angeles. Photo #N.30876)

Four generations of Corn clan: White Corn, Nampeyo's mother, in the center; Nampeyo on the right; Nampeyo's eldest daughter, Annie Healing, on the left, holding her first child, Rachel.

But George H. Pepper, who had also witnessed the Snake ceremony in an earlier year, purchased twenty-two bowls and seed jars from the potter.[4] Many of Pepper's vessels differ in character from those photographed by Vroman that same month. A few of the bowls are painted with Nampeyo's bold hand (Plate 3), but the other bowls and small jars are decorated with more simplistic designs suggestive of Annie's work (Plate 4).

That extraordinary August of 1901, forty-four vessels in two disparate groups were documented: twenty-two in Vroman's photographs and twenty-two in Pepper's collection. I asked one of Nampeyo's granddaughters if, under any circumstances, she would have had that many pieces of her work available at one time. "Yes," she answered, "if they hadn't sold." Aware of the increasing numbers of visitors attending the Snake ceremonies in 1895, 1897, and 1899, Nampeyo knew there would be an even larger number passing the house at the top of the trail in 1901. During the quiet preceding months, Nampeyo and Annie made their finest vessels to offer for sale when crowds ascended the mesa.

George A. Dorsey explained in a promotional booklet written for the Santa Fe Railway: "During the greater part of the year, [the villages] are left in almost seclusion," but, during August, they "begin to change, for the tourist and scientist throng the street of these quaint towns all eager to gain admission to the kiva and more eager on the final day to obtain an advantageous point of view on one of the terraces where they may snap their kodaks at a line of picturesquely dressed dancers and carry away the picture of a naked priest with a rattlesnake in his mouth."[5] He advised readers that the most skillful potters lived in Hano, "while the ware of old Nampeyo and her daughter have gone far and wide over the curio-loving world."[6] Even museum representatives employed colorful rhetoric. Did Dorsey characterize forty-year-old Nampeyo as "old" to make her more picturesque? Or to make her less formidable to prospective tourists?

The Snake Dance in 1903 attracted painter E. Irving Couse, whose paintings of Indians were reproduced on twenty-two calendars publicizing the Santa Fe Railway. Couse spent six weeks in Hopi, sketching and photographing the Snake ceremonies in Walpi and Mishongnovi and the Flute ceremony in Oraibi. While he worked, his wife, Virginia, and nine-year-old son, Kibbey, often walked from the house they occupied in Walpi through the middle village to visit Nampeyo in Hano. "Nampeyo was a good friend of ours," Virginia wrote to her sister. "We use[d] to go almost every day, Kibbey and I, and watch her make pottery and decorate it."[7] When the Couses left the mesa to settle permanently in Taos, they carried one of Nampeyo's pots with them (Plate 5).[8]

In the following year, 1904, Mary Colter made a personal collection of Nampeyo's work. Colter had been hired by the Fred Harvey Company in 1902 to decorate the Indian Building adjoining the new Alvarado Hotel in Albuquerque. She continued supervising construction of the Harvey empire for forty years, sometimes with abrasive authority but with unfailing good taste. Her collection included five bowls and two jars characteristic of both Nampeyo's (Plate 21) and Annie's work.[9]

Another documented collection was made in 1904 by Ole Solberg of the Ethnographic Museum of Oslo, Norway. Solberg had traveled to the Southwest to make an extensive collection of Hopi artifacts for the museum, which included eleven vessels made by Nampeyo. Three were nontraditional items: a little pitcher and two rather whimsical "sugar jars." The eight bowls, however, were of traditional inward-rolled-rim shape, painted with bold interior designs that were more geometric, more "patterned" than her usual flowing style. Three of the bowls were painted with random bands against an intricate "tweed" background that covered the entire interior surface of the bowls (Plate 20). The designs are markedly dissimilar to her other work, and to my knowledge, were never repeated.[10]

The Snake ceremony that attracted so many visitors in odd-numbered years to Walpi was held in Oraibi on Third Mesa in even-numbered years. Not as hospitable as Walpi, Oraibi did not attract as much publicity or as many visitors. Nevertheless, the Snake Dance in that pueblo was Jo Mora's destination when he left San Jose, California, in 1904, with a wagonful of photographic gear and watercolor materials.

Wearing boots, Levis, and an open-necked shirt, and with the black hair of his Spanish ancestors, he blended into the scene more naturally than his conservatively dressed peers in their suits and ties. During the ceremony, he met Elbridge Ayer Burbank, who had been roaming the Navajo and Hopi country drawing portraits, "redheads" they were called, with his red conté crayon. Burbank encouraged Mora to stay so they could work together. The invitation appealed to Mora, for Burbank knew the geography and understood the people.

The village of Polacca at the base of First Mesa, where they could obtain supplies at Pavatea's trading post, seemed a desirable place for the two artists to work. When they learned that they could rent Nampeyo's red-roofed stone house for a studio, they agreed to pay her five dollars a month.

The two settled in, buying chickens and eggs from the residents, hiring them to do their washing and to model for their sketches. With their easy manner, they developed a comfortable rapport with their subjects. Burbank asked Annie, "Quen-Chow-A,"[11] to sit for a portrait inside her house, but for reasons Burbank did not understand, she fainted while he was working. The astonished Burbank was trying to revive her when Nampeyo rushed outside and returned with a handful of sand that she rubbed over Annie's stomach. It seemed a strange remedy to Burbank, but Annie recovered immediately. Before he left in the spring, Burbank had drawn a "redhead" portrait of Nampeyo, also.[12]

After Burbank's departure, Mora stayed two more years in Nampeyo's stone house in Polacca. During that time he photographed Nampeyo and other residents, the villages, and ceremonies. Using watercolors, he painted a series of kachina studies[13] and the red trading post at the entrance to Keams Canyon. The painting of the post is inscribed "To the Boss of the ranch with remembrance of the best times ever. J.J. Mora /06."[14]

Jo Mora and the new young trader at Keams Canyon, Lorenzo Hubbell, Jr., became close friends. The post had been sold by Thomas Keam in 1902 to Juan Lorenzo Hubbell, who owned a trading post in Ganado. He sent his son, Lorenzo, Jr., to manage the Keams Canyon post, with its access to Hopi crafts. Shortly after purchasing the post, Lorenzo, Sr., compiled a catalog and price list, in which he stated, "What I tell you regarding these goods will be the truth, and you will in all cases find the prices based properly upon the value of the goods themselves, with no misrepresentations, no shams and no counterfeits."[15] The pamphlet described "Navajo Blankets & Indian Curios" available at both the Ganado post and the "Branch Store: Keam's Cañon, Arizona," and "Nanpea pottery; the only pottery that compares with the old in color, finish and design. But one squaw living knows the secret of making this pottery; from $0.50 to $10.00."[16]

Lorenzo, Sr., had been hired at the trading post in Ganado (located halfway between First Mesa and Gallup) one year after Thomas Keam had opened his trading post in Hopi. Two years later when he bought the Ganado post, Hubbell, affectionately known as Don Lorenzo, began a long and colorful career as a Navajo trader and art collector. In his ranch house behind the post, Hubbell welcomed politicians, military men, government representatives, photographers, and painters with whom he enthusiastically exchanged paintings for lodging.[17]

At the time he purchased the branch post, Hubbell began a mutually beneficial relationship with the Fred Harvey Company, which had established an Indian department under the direction of Herman Schweizer in 1902.[18] In this capacity, Schweizer sought the finest crafts, opened curio shops, and installed exhibits in Harvey hotels. Without legal authority to buy directly from Hopi craftsmen on the reservation, he purchased Hopi items wholesale from Don Lorenzo in Ganado, who obtained from them his son in Keams Canyon, who bought them directly from the makers on the mesas.

Utilizing empty boxcars returning to the East after hauling provisions to Harvey kitchens in the West, Schweizer filled them with native crafts from all the pueblos and reservations in the Southwest, creating new markets throughout the country. With Schweizer's astute business sense, the Fred Harvey Company became the first major commercial purveyor of Indian handcrafts. Mass marketing had begun.

Because of the new demand for quantities of crafts, interest in pottery-making was renewed on the mesas. The names and numbers of potters making "generic" Hopi pottery for the new markets outside the reservation remain unknown, but the Harvey people distinguished those items from pottery from other pueblos by identifying each piece with a little printed label glued to the bottom that read "From the Hopi Villages."[19]

With Nampeyo's work, however, a recognizable name could be marketed and, with the name, a higher price could be asked for the vessel. The Harvey Company identified her pieces with stickers that read "Made by Nampeyo, Hopi."

Hopi House

"Quaintly garbed Indians on the housetop."
—*Simpson,* El Tovar, A New Hotel
    at Grand Canyon of Arizona

Although many artists, scientists, and museum representatives were drawn west with a purpose, they did not fill the trains that left Chicago at ten o'clock every night. The Atchison Topeka & Santa Fe Railway, therefore, embarked on a campaign to lure vacationing travelers to the Southwest by means of photographs, paintings, calendars, picture books, and posters of the natives and the landscape. While individual photographers and artists worked on the mesas to depict residents in natural surroundings, countless unnamed photographers hired by the railway took "pretty" pictures for commercial exploitation. Shown by magic lantern, the hand-tinted glass slides presented a saccharine image of the Southwest.[1]

The campaign succeeded, and the job of making the passengers comfortable while traveling became the formidable task of the Fred Harvey Company. Harvey, a small energetic Englishman, convinced the railroad that it could establish an unprecedented reputation by offering fine dining and comfortable accommodations to its passengers, a convenience and luxury no competing railroad provided. In partnership, the Santa Fe built hotels and restaurants along the route and Fred Harvey managed them with a flair for meticulous service and exceptional food.

Those on board the nightly trains traveled through Kansas to Oklahoma, where, if they wished, they could break their journey by riding a stage into reservations of the Kaw, Tonkawa, Osage, Pawnee, Shawnee, Kickapoo, Cheyenne, Arapaho, Kiowa, and Comanche Indians. Back on board, they chugged toward the Rocky Mountains on the western horizon, across the Pecos River in New Mexico, to Lamy. They could depart again to take a short spur line to Santa Fe, where they could stroll the plaza amid Spanish-speaking people. Returning to the train at Lamy, they headed to one of two departure points in Arizona for the Hopi mesas. Livery stables in Holbrook and Winslow offered horses, wagons, and supplies for the two-day trip north to the Hopi villages.

In 1901, the Santa Fe Railway added another side trip for travelers along the route. The company bought a spur line that ran from Williams, west of Flagstaff on its main line, to a bankrupt copper mine at Anita, fifteen miles short of the Grand Canyon. Only a rustic hotel provided overnight accommodations at the canyon for visitors arriving by wagon from Flagstaff. Seeing the commercial possibilities of attracting travelers to a luxurious hotel at one of the world's most awesome natural phenomena, the railroad pushed completion of the line to the rim. On January 14, 1905, the new hotel officially opened with a flourish. Named after the explorer in Coronado's expedition who viewed the canyon in 1540, El Tovar was a rock-and-wooden structure of chalet style that provided eighty guest rooms with electric lights, several art galleries that sold the work of known artists who painted at the canyon, a music room, a solarium, and, of course, a fine dining room.

During construction of the hotel, the Harvey Company asked Mary Colter to design a building to be located nearby, where the guests could purchase curios and watch Indian craftsmen demonstrate their skills in weaving, basketry, pottery- and jewelry-making. To advise her, the Harvey people hired Mennonite missionary and Hopi scholar H.R. Voth.

Colter drew plans for a three-story terraced structure characteristic of a cluster of Hopi dwellings with typical pole ladders to each terrace. Constructed entirely by Hopi workmen, the sixty-by-ninety-foot building consisted of small plastered rooms with corner fireplaces on the first floor for displaying handwoven rugs, kachina dolls, jewelry, pottery, baskets,

Mexican crafts and antiques, totem poles and Northwest Coast Indian crafts, as well as items from many tribes and pueblos.

The second floor housed the growing ethnological collection of the Fred Harvey Company, which included priceless old Navajo blankets, baskets, rare buffalo-hide shields, and reproductions of two Hopi altars made by Voth. The third floor provided residence for the manager and his family. Living quarters that were separated from the public rooms on the first and second floors were provided for native craftsmen brought from the Navajo and Moqui reservations to demonstrate their crafts.

John F. Huckel, Fred Harvey's son-in-law who assumed management of the company after Harvey's death, took charge of the opening of Hopi House. After initial contacts and procedures had been established, requests for Hopi craftsmen to go to the canyon originated from Herman Schweizer to Don Lorenzo Hubbell at Ganado or to his son Lorenzo, Jr., at Keams Canyon or directly to the superintendent of the Moqui

16. "An Indian Living Room, Hopi House." William Henry Jackson, 1905. (Colorado Historical Society, Photo #WHJ18137)

In private living quarters at Hopi House, Grand Canyon, son William sits at the loom, Lesso smokes in front of the fire, and Nampeyo holds a bowl with others in the background. The children are probably Wesley, standing, and Fannie, seated.

Agency. The superintendent in turn passed the requests to the principal teachers of the day schools at each mesa.

To Schweizer's frustration, Hopi craftsmen did not always answer his calls for volunteers. Winter could be ruthlessly cold on the mesa tops, and the prospect of being comfortably housed at the canyon was enhanced by the prospect of selling work to tourists. So many volunteered during the winter months that Schweizer kept a file of names for future reference. Spring and summer, however, were seasons for planting, followed by the fall harvest when each member of the family shared the work to ensure full storage rooms for the coming year. Frantically, Schweizer would pressure the Hubbells and then the superintendent for craftsmen to replace those who wanted to go home. The superintendent, in turn, urged the teachers to find parties who were willing to leave their fields. With no volunteers coming forth, the superintendent would attempt to placate Schweizer by explaining that he had never seen a people as dedicated to working in the fields as the Hopis were.

Although Navajos expressed enthusiasm for staying at the canyon, Schweizer and Huckel were committed to the original concept of Hopi House: to present Hopi Indians in an authentic background to a curious public. "The Hopi House filled with Navajo Indians is inconsistent," Huckel complained. "I know it is more difficult to handle Hopis, but it seems to me with an interpreter this can be arranged without their giving too much trouble. Will you take this matter up promptly . . ."[2] At one point, Huckel entered the negotiations directly, asking Hubbell, "When will they have their corn put up and when do you think they could go? . . . If I came out would I be able to hurry them up, do you think?[3]

Supplying clay to the potters presented another problem. Hopi potters would work only with their own clay, which meant carrying enough with them or, if it became depleted, having new supplies transported to them. When Schweizer sent clay from Acoma to them, they refused to use it "for some reason"[4] and asked to go home. If they could not make pots, they could not make money, which was their motivation for staying. Other excuses prompted sudden departures of entire families: their house on the mesa had fallen in; their burros had run away; their possessions had been stolen. The difficulty of controlling the independent Hopis caused Schweizer to explode like others before him. "I think the Hopis are 'hoodoos!'"[5]

Transporting groups of Hopis and Tewas to Grand Canyon involved complex arrangements and cooperation between the Harvey Company, the Santa Fe Railway, the superintendent of the Moqui Agency, Don Lorenzo Hubbell, and Lorenzo, Jr. From his trading post in Ganado, Don Lorenzo sent wagons to his son's post at Keams Canyon to collect the families and everything they might need for temporary residence away from mesa life: raw materials to demonstrate their craft, clothes, kachina dolls, dance accessories, and so on. They and their belongings were transported to Ganado where they spent the night, and then to Gallup the following day. Transferred to the train in charge of a Santa Fe Railway representative, they traveled to Williams, where, again, they were transferred to the spur line going north to the canyon. After they arrived at Hopi House, the Harvey Company agreed to give them a warm place to live, suitable food, and satisfactory prices for items they made. Some families stayed the two or three months that the Harvey Company requested. Others, unable to adapt, returned home as soon as permission was granted. Transporting them home entailed making reverse arrangements with the railroad and Don Lorenzo.

The responsibility of engaging the first group of Hopis to leave their homes, to travel by wagon and by train, to demonstrate their crafts to canyon visitors, to be absent during traditional mesa ceremonies apparently fell to Lorenzo, Jr., who discussed the problem with his new friend Jo Mora.[6] Mora suggested that if Nampeyo were convinced to go others might follow. Nampeyo had frequently demonstrated her work for visitors who bought her pots and photographed her, and she was not reluctant to communicate with them through an interpreter. The proposal must have appealed to Nampeyo, for the family prepared to leave the mesa for the opening of Hopi House planned for Christmas of 1904.

The official opening was delayed, however, until January

1, 1905. Before the house was occupied, H. R. Voth had inspected the building and telegraphed Huckel that it was too cold and damp to house the Indians. Huckel postponed the departure of Nampeyo's family from Keams Canyon until December 26 and asked Hubbell to delay them for another day or two at Ganado. They finally arrived at Grand Canyon the evening of January 7, 1905, and "when they saw the Hopi Pueblo they cried 'Lolomei!'"[7] expressing their approval.

The group consisted of four men, two women, and five children.[8] Only Nampeyo and Lesso were named in correspondence, but reference was made to Annie and Willie Healing, and to the two adult sons of Nampeyo and Lesso, Kaloakuno and William. We can assume that the children were Nampeyo's ten-year-old daughter, Nellie, five-year-old son, Wesley, and her youngest, Fannie; also Annie and Willie's young Rachel. Annie's second child, Daisy, had not yet been born, so the fifth child is unknown.

I [Daisy] almost born there. Just when my mother come back from there in about a week time I was born. (1982)

With their well-known attraction in residence, Harvey's promotional brochures featured photographs of Nampeyo and her family on one of the terraces of Hopi House. The accompanying statement read: "These quaintly-garbed Indians on the housetop hail from Tewa, the home of Nampeyo, the most noted pottery-maker in all Hopiland. Perhaps you [will be] so fortunate as to see Nampeyo herself."[9] The brochures invited guests to "Go inside and you see how these gentle folk live. The rooms are little and low, like their small statured occupants. The Hopis are making 'piki,' twining the raven black hair of the 'manas' in big side whorls, smoking corncob pipes, building sacred altars, mending moccasins—doing a hundred un-American things. They are the most primitive Indians in America, with ceremonies several centuries old."[10]

In the evenings when a sufficient number of visitors had gathered, the men gave a few brief dances and songs that, the brochure explained, faintly suggested the style of some of their more elaborate ceremonials. After the dance, observers customarily threw money to the dancers, but a Harvey rule

did not allow direct solicitation by Indians among the guests.

A few days after Nampeyo's arrival, Huckel wrote to Hubbell in Ganado that the family had brought only two small boxes of clay for Nampeyo's work, and she was anxious to have more. He thought Tom Polacca might know where to dig for it and asked Hubbell to have half a dozen boxes of the clay taken to his post to be shipped by the regular route. The clay no doubt arrived in time to keep Nampeyo working, for her pottery sold well, as did other Hopi crafts: plaques, baskets, and, surprising to Huckel, sashes and embroidered kilts.

While she was working at Hopi House, Nampeyo produced some unusual round "discs," fourteen to fifteen inches in diameter, "simply big platters . . . almost flat, except a slight sloping up at the edges."[11] Apparently she had difficulty with the clay or in the firing, for several of them broke. Huckel bought the few that were perfect and two years later ordered more, asking her to use some of her best old designs. He also asked her to make some ten-inch-square Hopi plaques to be set in a mantelpiece in a new Harvey building at Ash Fork, west of Williams.

17. "Native Roof Garden Party, The Hopi House." Unknown, 1905. (University of Arizona Library Special Collections Department. Photo #11,027)

The Fred Harvey Company used this photo of Nampeyo and her family to publicize Hopi House, Grand Canyon. From left to right: Nampeyo, Annie, Nampeyo's son William (standing), and Lesso. The four seated children are probably Nampeyo's youngest child Fannie, Annie's first child Rachel, and Nampeyo's son Wesley and daughter Nellie.

Nampeyo and Lesso, Annie and Willie, the two adult sons, and all the children remained at Hopi House for three months and were transported home only after a test of wills with the Harvey people. The family wanted to plant corn in their fields by the first of April. Huckel did not want them to leave until another group could replace them. He wrote urgently to Lorenzo, Jr., requesting him to find a couple of pottery-makers and their husbands as soon as possible, and to Don Lorenzo, asking when it would be convenient for his wagon teams to meet Nampeyo and her family in Gallup to return them to the mesa. Belatedly, he wrote to Superintendent Lemmon of the Moqui Agency, expressing the hope that the superintendent would not object to the Harvey Company's taking a group of Hopis from the mesas to Grand Canyon occasionally. Three days later, Huckel sent a more emphatic note to Don Lorenzo, telling him to set a date immediately for meeting the group in Gallup. The Hopis were getting restive.

They returned by train to Williams, transferred to a train to Gallup, rode by wagon to Ganado, and then back to Keams Canyon. As a young man, Edmund Nequatewa[12] mingled with a large crowd gathered around the family to hear tales of their experiences at the new Hopi House. Two weeks later, Lorenzo, Jr., asked Nequatewa himself to accompany another group to Grand Canyon, but, as the wagon waited, they changed their minds and refused to leave. Three months passed before two families from Hano agreed to go, with Nequatewa joining them as interpreter.

When the second group arrived at Hopi House and saw the exceptional pottery that Nampeyo had made while she was there, the two women potters felt ashamed of their own skills. Nequatewa encouraged them, imploring them to try. In a memoir written many years later, he recalled that "the two women made up their minds and went to work, in no time they were puting [sic] out some good work, but of course these can not be call [sic] Nampeyo." And then in tribute to the old lady he added that Nampeyo had worked hard to make her reputation, "so with her effort she has uplifted her people to where they are now making good pottery."[13]

Children

"They were a nice couple, her and Lesso." (1986)

During the early twentieth century, collections of Indian artifacts in museums burgeoned, but as more expeditions were sent into the field to excavate more ruins for more treasures, leaders of the archaeological teams reported that vandalism and unskilled pot-hunters had destroyed many prehistoric sites. In a report written after the Museum-Gates Expedition in 1901, Walter Hough blamed early settlers, professional looters, and "almost every trader [who] either employed Indians to dig or bought all the specimens that Indians brought in at a nominal price."[1]

In 1905, the commissioner of Indian affairs warned traders to cease dealing in relics, threatening revocation of their licenses if they did not comply. The following year, Congress passed the Antiquities Act in an effort to inhibit further destruction of ancient sites on federal property. Only by permission of the secretaries of the interior, agriculture, and army could excavations and the gathering of antiquities be undertaken to benefit reputable museums, universities, colleges, or other educational institutions. Unauthorized persons collecting at ancient sites would, upon conviction, be fined and/or imprisoned. The act has since been revised, but apprehension and prosecution of violators has proved nearly impossible. Countless isolated ruins cannot be patrolled, and the chance of finding a looter with shovel in one hand and a relic in the other is remote.

While the government in Washington conceived laws to protect material artifacts, Oraibi on Third Mesa had split between conservative "Hostiles" who objected to outside interference and progressive "Friendlies" who were more tolerant. Bitter dispute divided families and clans. On September 8, 1906, the Friendlies forced every Hostile to the edge of town, where they were told to leave in order to preserve peace. The Hostiles refused, saying that they were the true practitioners of Hopi tradition and had the right to remain in their own village. Someone suggested a shoving match to determine which faction should leave and which could remain.

A line was drawn. Supporters pushed behind their leaders. The Hostiles lost, gathered their belongings, and turned their backs on their homes and the pueblo. They settled a few miles northwest of Oraibi near Hotevilla Spring, without food or shelter but with their beliefs uncompromised. With determination, they built the village of Hotevilla, carrying on their ceremonies without their traditional religious objects, which had been left behind.

Taking advantage of the turmoil, a Mennonite convert in Oraibi set fire to many such objects, which he found abhorrent, including two altars. "So neither the Oraibis nor the Hotevillas had the sacred objects any more. . . . The continuity was broken."[2]

Unconcerned by turmoil among factions on Third Mesa, the Tewas on First Mesa had settled into a peaceful compromise with the intrusions of government representatives, of school authorities, of missionaries, and of visitors in increasing numbers. After being the public attraction at Hopi House for three months, Nampeyo and her family returned to their mesa home, no doubt eager to resume familiar routines. The men planted their corn and other crops at Sand Hill ranch, and Nampeyo once again dug clay for pottery and carried water from the spring. When Annie gave birth to her second child, Daisy, a room was darkened for twenty days.

My grandma had friends, white people. They bring her cloth and sometimes instead of using it for the clay, "I'm going to make a blanket, a quilt," and she make the quilt out of it. "I have a big family and I have to give them blankets," is what she say. (1982)

18. "Nampeyo (the noted Hopi pottery maker) and her grandchild." Photographer and date unknown. (Denver Public Library, Western History Department. Photo #F47148)

This print was made from a tinted postcard bearing the above caption. I question whether the photo was taken after 1901, however, when Nampeyo's first grandchild was born. Her features are younger; the same necklace is seen on Annie in Matteson's photo of the late-1890s (Photograph 11) and Vroman's photographs of 1901 (Photographs 14 and 15). The bowl is similar in shape and interior design to bowls ca. 1900. The wide-eyed child may have been one of her own.

Nampeyo loved to tell stories to the children, some that she made up, others about the ancient ones.

We little ones would sit there with our mouths open listening. (1988)

Long ago, she would tell them, when the people wanted to get rid of ants, they made little ant pots into which they put honey. They placed the pots near ant hills, and the sweet honey attracted the ants. When all the ants were eating the honey, the people used a stick or hoe to move the pot far away so the ants could not bite the children any more.

When the ants weren't running to and fro working, Nampeyo told them, they had their celebrations, too. In their little village underground, they met and agreed to have a special dance. They dressed up in little bird feathers and the wings of butterflies. For moccasins, they wore the shoes that people left about. They had a fine time.

Storytellers always attracted children, and many little ones gathered around the Corn clan dwellings: Nampeyo's own, her grandchildren, and friends of them all.

> We like to go there 'cause they were a nice couple, her and Lesso. (1986)

Nampeyo always had a basket filled with dried peaches to pass out to the children.

> She dried them on rocks, on the roof, wherever she could find a place to dry, but too much work. Every breeze [she] take [them] inside so it doesn't get too much dust. She put them in jar sunk in the floor with cover. She made large storage jars. Decorated? They don't need any decoration on those 'cause they'll be buried in the ground. (1986)

Despite activities of household and family, Nampeyo continued to make her pottery, undecorated utensils for domestic use and decorated vessels to trade. Some of the bowls and jars she carried down the trail to Tom Pavatea's trading post. After a cursory examination at the counter, Tom would smile and ask her what she wanted in trade.

> She would pick out everything she wanted and then at the end she would ask, "Do I have any money left?" He always said "Yes," so she would bring candy back for the children. (1983)

Gathering a small flock about her one day, Nampeyo took Fannie, Rachel, and Daisy through middle village to a Hopi dance held in Walpi. A sudden wind whipped around the exposed plaza with such a frenzy that the dancers had to stop. Afraid that she and the three small ones would be blown off the narrow path connecting Walpi to the middle village, Nampeyo sought shelter in a house in Walpi until the wind subsided. Finally, with Daisy secured to her back by a shawl and holding the hands of Fannie on one side and Rachel on the other, Nampeyo made her way across the narrow path, back through Sichomovi and the plaza of Hano, to the family dwelling. They arrived late and tired from what was to have been a brief excursion.

It was a hard time but it was a good life. Everybody's taking care of themselves. My grandma, she didn't like to go away. She would go to ranch one night and come home. She wanted to stay home. (1986)

Chicago

"Nampeyjo, squaw, the greatest maker of Indian pottery alive."
      —Chicago Sunday Tribune

The concept of merely inviting craftsmen to participate in activities at Hopi House was not evident in letters written by J.F. Huckel and Herman Schweizer of the Fred Harvey Company. They expected mesa residents to leave their homes willingly upon request and to stay at Hopi House until replacements for them could be found. Hopi women were required to make baskets and pottery for sale, and Hopi men, in addition to weaving, were compelled "to work around the store, pack and clean up, etc. and to help the dance along at night."[1] Neither Huckel nor Schweizer was tolerant of indecision and delays, nor did they understand that Hopis viewed their pressure for craftsmen to leave their homes not as an opportunity but as another intrusion into their lives.

The Harvey people exploited Nampeyo's reputation in publicizing Hopi House, but they were ambivalent about wanting her to return. She was a strong individual, not intimidated by white people, dedicated to a tradition they did not understand. Reluctantly, they had let her family leave Hopi House in the spring of 1905 to return home to plant their corn. In September, John Huckel contacted Don Lorenzo in Ganado about having the family return, but he expressed reservations. He was impatient that "Nampeyo's party was pretty independent and pretty much spoiled. . . . They did not want to do anything unless they were paid for it."[2] He conceded that "Nampeyo and her daughter are excellent pottery makers and this may overcome any other objections, yet it occurred to me it might be well for me or someone from our concern to see these people and have a distinct understanding before they left, though possibly it may not be necessary."[3]

In October, Huckel had decided that Nampeyo and her family should return and asked Don Lorenzo which family members might accompany her. He presumed there would be Lesso, Willie and Annie, and the two little infants (no doubt Fannie and Rachel), although he may not have known that Daisy had been born to Annie since their first trip to the canyon. Nellie and Wesley, he speculated, might have to stay behind to attend school. Nampeyo's two older sons, who had not been happy at Grand Canyon, probably would want to accompany the family, nevertheless. If the sons chose not to go, Huckel thought that two or three more men should be included in the group to make up a complement of at least five men.

In December, Huckel wrote to Superintendent Lemmon, requesting that the whole family be allowed to go to Hopi House, and to Hubbell in Ganado, asking him to provide transportation as soon as possible. In a conciliatory mood, he added that the family would know "about what to expect and they know that whatever we tell them we will do, we will carry out."[4] A second letter to Hubbell stated that he had not yet received Superintendent Lemmon's agreement to his request, but he reiterated that he wanted Nampeyo, Lesso, Willie and Annie, the two boys, and such other children as would be allowed to accompany them. As reassurance he added, "You might tell them that a new roof was put on the Hopi House in the spring and that their rooms in the Hopi House will be perfectly warm and dry; that they will be supplied with warm bedding, good food, etc."[5]

In mid-January, however, another group, not the Nampeyo family, was transported from Hopi to the Grand Canyon. That was perfectly satisfactory to Huckel. A year passed. In early January 1907, after further correspondence about Nampeyo, she agreed to return. However, when she postponed leaving, perhaps again, Hubbell arranged for another group to go instead. In frustration, Huckel suggested that some Oraibi families be approached, as he felt that they were not as "spoiled" as the residents of Hano and Walpi.

Herman Schweizer, who had assumed responsibility for recruiting craftsmen for Hopi House, learned in early February that Nampeyo "with 2 children, and another woman with 3 children, and Tom Polacca's wife with 2 children, and the Wheel Girl . . . and also four men"[6] were ready to return to Grand Canyon. Whereas Huckel felt that children were the greatest attraction, Schweizer wanted men, few women, and no more children than necessary. Responding to Hubbell, he stated repeatedly and bluntly that he wanted as few women and children as possible. He thought that four men, two women, and the wheel girl would make an attractive group.

The Harvey-Hubbell correspondence did not discuss Nampeyo's second stay at Hopi House or name members of the family that accompanied her. Annie's second child, Daisy, would have been two years old at that time.

> *I [Daisy] was still a baby so I really don't know what happened there. When I was coming back my uncles were carrying me around and "What is it that brought you?" "That's a bucket," I said. "What did you ride on coming home?" "A bucket." In Tewa, [the word* train*] almost sound like a bucket. They used to tease me. (1982)*

A letter of panic from Schweizer to Hubbell stated that all the Hopis wanted to leave at once on account of sickness at home. The date, April 5, suggestively coincided with the planting of corn. Their departure, he said, would leave Hopi House without a single Indian. "Shriners excursions will be at the Canyon towards the end of this month . . . over one thousand at the Canyon in one day so we must have Indians."[7]

Nampeyo's presence had contributed authenticity to Hopi House, but she also had benefited in reputation. To satisfy the growing demand for her pottery, she made more bowls that were less expensive and easier for travelers to carry home. Schweizer, who bought from the traders for resale by the Harvey Company, became increasingly critical of both the quality and price of her work. "If you have any Nampayo bowls," a typed letter to Don Lorenzo Hubbell in 1908 stated, "will be glad to have you make a shipment of about two or three dozen." He then added to the order in bold script, "good ones only."[8] A follow-up letter indicated that Hubbell had raised the price of the bowls to seventy-five cents, irritating Schweizer, who complained that the trader was getting like the Indians, raising prices on those items that were most in demand.

Finally, in 1910, Superintendent Horton Miller granted "Mr. Huckel's request for permission to send a representative to this reservation for the purpose of procuring Indian curios."[9] He warned the Harvey Company, however, that excavating the ruins or purchasing artifacts taken from the ruins was forbidden by law.

From the stone house on the mesa, Nampeyo's pots traveled to many places unknown to their maker. Illustrated brochures and publications featured her picture and the name that she herself could neither read nor write. Sometime before 1910, after White Corn had died, Nampeyo became the saja of the family, but unlike all Corn clan sajas before her, the fifty-year-old potter had traveled from her mesa home twice and did so once again. Taking with her boxes of clay with which to demonstrate her skills, she journeyed fifteen hundred miles across the country to the city of Chicago.

During the late 1800s and early 1900s, numerous expositions were financed in metropolitan areas to display the tools and products of industrial progress along with the optimistic message of the future growth of the country. Concerned about high food prices and short supplies in the burgeoning cities of the Northeast, the *Chicago Tribune* sponsored a Land Show in 1909 to encourage more intensive farming of agricultural lands in the South and the West. The exposition drew such enthusiastic crowds that the *Tribune* together with the unified business community of Chicago sponsored a second United States Land and Irrigation Exposition, which was held in the Chicago Coliseum in 1910.

Organizers of such expositions did not overlook the impact on the public of exhibits of modern machinery contrasted with the still "primitive" lifestyles of native cultures. Seeking a direct benefit that would promote travel to the Southwest, the Santa Fe Railway hired George A. Dorsey of the Field Museum and Herman Schweizer of the Fred Harvey Company to design a brown stucco mission building that would be inhabited for the duration of the Land Show by Hopi Indians.

Three months before its opening, John F. Huckel of the Harvey Company initiated a request to take Hopis to Chicago in a letter to Superintendent Horton H. Miller of the Moqui Agency.[10] By October, specific plans and terms for their participation had been proposed by Herman Schweizer, who requested one family from Oraibi and one from Second Mesa, the women of each to make baskets, and a third family from First Mesa to make pottery. Only two children should accompany each family, and two men must be blanket-makers or weavers of kilts and sashes. Making certain that they fulfilled their roles as "Indians," he stated that the girls should have their hair done in "whorls," that all men should wear moccasins, velvet shirts, and bandanas around their foreheads, and that the women should wear their native costumes. One member of the group should be able to speak English to act as interpreter.

The financial arrangement was to be the same as that at Hopi House. All travel and living expenses would be paid, and the craftsmen would be paid for the items that they made at the Coliseum. "It will not be possible to bake any pottery in the building. They will simply mould it, and we will, of course, throw it away, unless we can get some of it baked in Chicago. We will, of course, pay them for whatever pottery they make, even if they don't bake it; but," Schweizer added, "all these details are of a minor consideration."[11]

On November 12, Nampeyo and Lesso, their daughter Nellie, who was about sixteen years old, and Nellie's friend Ida Avayo left First Mesa by wagon for the train bound for Chicago, taking with them all the paraphernalia necessary for the occasion. They carried dance ornaments for Lesso and kachina dolls: "The Indians were engaged yesterday in putting in place scores of wonderfully wrought and colored idols called 'Katcina.'"[12] They also carried clay for "Nampeyjo, squaw, regarded as the greatest maker of Indian pottery alive.

She is frequently consulted by the eminent scientists of the country with reference to what she knows about pottery making. Lasso, a famous Indian dancer, is with the party."[13]

When Secretary of Agriculture James Wilson officially opened the show on November 19, he stressed the need for development in the South and West and irrigation projects throughout the country. Booths displaying produce from all states filled the coliseum; a model farm exhibited modern equipment; a mammoth topographical picture showed construction work for completion of the Panama Canal. A pictorial representation of Yellowstone Falls covered one end inside the building and a picture of Yosemite Valley the other. Blue bunting stretched over the entire interior overhead to simulate the sky. And three specially cast bells over the entrance to the Santa Fe Railway mission rang out at intervals during the day.

In its two-page article headlined "LAND SHOW IS ON," the *Chicago Sunday Tribune* praised the wonder pomegranates and mammoth raisins, the pestless apples and twenty-five-pound sweet potatoes. It mentioned the Russian Band and the Hawaiian singers, but Nampeyo and Lesso were the only participants identified by name.

Nampeyo, Lesso, Nellie, and Ida had departed by train from Winslow and, after the show, were returned there by the Santa Fe Railway.[14] They completed the journey by wagon toward the low flat mesas on the northern horizon, where Nampeyo remained for the rest of her life.

Her brother Tom, who had been forced to move with his family from their house in Polacca to the security of the ranch, continued to lead an active life and to inculcate in his children the principles of his Mormon faith. On September 6, 1910, Superintendent Horton H. Miller wrote a letter of introduction, addressed "To Whom Presented," giving Polacca "[who is] a policeman under this jurisdiction . . . permission to visit among the Pueblos in New Mexico for the purpose of trading with them."[15] Eight months later, on May 11, 1911, Polacca died, apparently of pneumonia. He was buried in an unmarked grave somewhere in the hills.

Twenty-nine years after his death, Polacca's church commemorated his unwavering religious faith by placing a stone marker at the ranch. The bronze plaque reads in part: "Official Marker, Utah Pioneer Trails and Landmarks Association, Church of Jesus Christ of Latter-day Saints, Erected June 16, 1940. Tom Polacca, linguist, trader, rancher, social and religious advocate . . . 1853–1911."[16] The evening before the monument was dedicated, Tom's descendants gathered around a campfire at the ranch to sing and to talk. His faith and his spirit enveloped them. Four elders representing the church baptized all of Polacca's descendants who were present.

A more public tribute was paid to Tom Polacca during his lifetime in the 1893 Extra Census Bulletin of the Eleventh Census of the United States:

> It would be an injustice to a good and worthy man should I fail to make favorable mention of the Indian of Tewa who devoted his time so generously in the height of the harvest season to our interests, who has forsaken the home of his fathers and many of their ways by moving his home down from the mesa and breaking away from many of the customs and superstitions of his tribe, thereby invoking the anathemas of his people; a man whose highest ambition is to learn and adopt the ways of the white man in all things (excepting possibly the vices). It is with profound respect and admiration of a good, true, and brave man that I commend to the fostering care and generous treatment of those who have charge of the nation's wards the big, kindhearted Tom Polacca.[17]

After Polacca's death, Annie and her family moved from the Corn clan dwellings on the mesa to the simple stone houses at Sand Hill so Annie's husband, Willie, could tend the ranch. Annie frequently returned to the Corn clan house, however, to make pottery alongside her mother, and one or more of her children were always there. When it was time for them to begin their schooling, Rachel, Daisy, Dewey, Fletcher, Beatrice, and Lucy in succession returned to live at their grandmother's house, from which they hiked the trail to the schoolhouse below. Dewey explained that the children

> *stayed with Lesso and Nampeyo and an uncle and another uncle. My mother and dad stayed way out with sheep and cattle.* (1986)

Reminiscing about those early days, Daisy recalled,

> At that time we go to school about seven years old and my
> sister [Rachel] is about eight or nine years old and Fannie is
> about nine or ten. I was only five or six years old and I
> always follow my sister Rachel. When she goes to school, I
> go with her. The teacher told me I'm not old enough to go
> to school, but anyway I just follow my sister around. The
> teacher used to get me paper and pencil and I be sitting on
> the side. I learned English first. She just talk to the other
> children and before you know it . . . (1982)

During the first decade of the twentieth century, Nampeyo
was potting prolifically and masterfully. Before photographs
brought recognition, Nampeyo displayed magnificent vessels
on a rug in front of her house. By the end of the decade, her
production was purchased for resale by Lorenzo, Jr., at his
Keams Canyon trading post, by Lorenzo, Sr., at his post in
Ganado, and by representatives of the Fred Harvey Company.
But she always kept some vessels to carry down the trail to
Tom Pavatea's trading post in Polacca to barter for provisions
for her growing family.

Published Distortions

"Distant ignorance and lack of sympathy."
    —*Crane*, Indians of the Enchanted Desert

When Dr. Samuel A. Barrett, director of the Milwaukee Public Museum, traveled to the Moqui Reservation in 1911 to record ceremonies and observe craft techniques, he made a comprehensive documentation of Nampeyo at work and a collection of her vessels. At his request, she made a group of partially coiled models, setting each aside at succeeding stages as she progressed to illustrate how a vessel is shaped from start to finish. Barrett recorded her method of work and took a sequential series of photographs of Nampeyo shaping and painting a jar. When he returned to the museum, he took with him the series of unfinished pots, samples of clay, paints, yucca brushes, polishing stones, and other implements. He also made a fine collection of twenty-two of her vessels that varied from small seed jars and bowls to large water jars and canteens.[1]

Although early in the century Annie had received considerable recognition as an excellent potter from outsiders, including Samuel Barrett, no extant vessels of that period are attributed to her. They may have been purchased by visitors merely as attractive Hopi souvenirs, and many unknowingly were included in collections of Nampeyo's work.

Among the earliest vessels directly attributed to Annie were those purchased in 1912 by artist William R. Leigh. Leigh had traveled west to paint landscapes for the Santa Fe Railway in 1906, but finding attractive figurative subject matter

19. "Nampeyo painting a pot." Samuel A. Barrett, 1911. (Milwaukee Public Museum. Photo #6644)

Dr. Barrett made a large collection of Nampeyo's pottery (Photograph 20) and took a series of photographs of her making vessels. In this photo, Nampeyo is seated outside her house; the ladder protruding from the Pendete Kiva is seen behind her. (One of eleven photographs.)

among the natives, he returned to the Southwest frequently for the next twenty years. In 1912, Leigh accepted the hospitality of Don Lorenzo in Ganado, and at the Hubbell ranch house he met sculptor Emry Kopta and painter Lon Megargee. The three sketched together on the Navajo Reservation and then moved on to Polacca, where they rented a red-roofed government house from one of the Hopi women.

Leigh sketched incessantly, occasionally hiking the trail to the top of the mesa after midnight to paint by moonlight. He was attracted to Annie and painted several portraits of her. When he returned to his studio in New York, he took with him vessels made by both mother (Plate 9) and daughter. Three of them—a red-slipped jar (Plate 10), a white-slipped globose jar, and a large storage jar—were marked "Made by daughter of Nam-pa-ya Tawa 1st Mesa, Ariz. 1912." A fourth appears in a preliminary charcoal drawing on canvas of Annie surrounded by several vessels.[2] All are expertly crafted, demonstrating Annie's maturity as a potter. Had Leigh not identified them, all could be mistaken for her mother's work.

William R. Leigh and Lon Megargee left Polacca after several months of work, but Emry Kopta remained. An Austrian who had lost a leg in a ranch accident, Kopta was a musician, amateur photographer, and sculptor. Extending an affection for this gentle man, Tom Pavatea embraced Kopta as one of his own, providing him with a corner room of the new house he had built for his growing family. Pavatea also prepared a building next to his trading post for Kopta to use as a studio. In return, the sculptor assisted Pavatea in the store whenever he was needed. The residents grew accustomed to the man who walked with a stiff gait through their villages singing kachina songs, and they willingly posed for sculpted portraits and for photographs of personal and ceremonial activities.

With clay as his medium, Kopta felt a kinship to Nampeyo, who had mastered its use. Because the commercial clay Kopta used was expensive and difficult to obtain, Nampeyo shared her source of natural clay with him, teaching him how to work it into a malleable consistency. She also taught him how to fire his work with sheep dung and coal in the tradition of

20. Collection of Nampeyo pottery at the Milwaukee Public Museum. (Milwaukee Public Museum. Photo #XE–482–13E)

In 1911, Dr. Samuel A. Barrett, then director of the museum, made an extensive collection of Nampeyo's vessels and pottery-making tools. The collection is on permanent display at the museum, illustrated by Barrett's photographs of Nampeyo at work.

21. "Nampaya, Hopi pottery maker, seated with work." Joseph K. Dixon, 1913. (Mathers Museum, Indiana University. Photo #W3279)

In 1908, 1909, and 1913, Dixon made major photographic expeditions to record North American Indians. His visit to the Hopi Reservation produced one of the last extensive bodies of photographs of the Hopis before the elders banned photographers from further work. The circular motif and stylized kachina design on the jar on the left side of the photograph were painted by Nampeyo during a short period ca. 1912–1915. (One of six images of Nampeyo and her pottery)

mesa potters. Kopta sculpted figures and busts of the chiefs of various societies, the medicine man, of Nampeyo's granddaughter Daisy, and in the course of their close relationship, Nampeyo herself sat for a sculpted portrait.[3]

Kopta documented Hopi life during World War I when few outsiders were present, but unfortunately, he did not date his photographs. The dates of a rare, full-face portrait of Nampeyo (Photograph 22) and another of her holding a pot (Photograph 24) can only be approximated. Other photographs recorded Tom Pavatea at his post, children at play, and families

22. Nampeyo. Emry Kopta, ca. 1915. (Museum of Northern Arizona. Photo #MS240–2–88)

Sculptor Emry Kopta lived in Polacca from 1912 to 1922. His photographs, unfortunately, were not dated, but comparing the potter's graying hair to other photos, I would judge this rare portrait to have been taken about 1915.

at their tasks planting corn, spinning yarn, carrying firewood, and collecting water at the spring. They are a rare pictorial record of daily life and ceremonial activities.[4]

While Nampeyo was sharing her clay and firing methods with Kopta, a young Hopi was courting her second daughter. Nellie's suitor, Douglas Douma, had wanted more skills than his school years had offered, so he had taken correspondence courses to learn typing and bookkeeping. Tom Pavatea employed him at his trading post, where Douma became an indispensable assistant and correspondent between Pavatea and the world outside the reservation.

Like others of the younger generation, Douma and Nellie moved into one of the houses at the bottom of the trail after their marriage to follow an independent life. Nellie gave birth to eight children, the first generation of the Corn clan not raised in the dwellings of their ancestors.

Nampeyo's youngest child, tempestuous Fannie, was the least compatible with her mother, and she married young.

Among the Hano Tewa, marriage was forbidden between people of certain relationships, such as two members of the same clan. Marriage was also forbidden between children of a brother and sister,[5] but Tom Polacca's youngest child, Vinton, and Nampeyo's youngest, Fannie, married, defying tradition. They raised their seven Corn clan children in the Mormon faith of their paternal grandfather.

The trading post at Keams Canyon changed hands a second time when, in 1914, Joseph Schmedding bought the business. Buildings erected by traders and improvements on existing buildings became government property, which could not be sold; only good will and inventory transferred to a new proprietor. Lorenzo, Jr., and Schmedding worked a week to estimate the merchandise stocked at the post in order to arrive at a satisfactory price for the sale.

Schmedding was overwhelmed by the quantity and variety of Hopi pottery that was stored in a large number of cases in a long, shedlike room. There were tens of thousands of pieces: "I never learned the exact amount. In size and shape they ranged from small pieces of finger-bowl shape to large ollas; others resembled punch bowls and urns, and many pieces were of tall vase-like appearance. Several large cases were filled completely with shallow, platelike plaques. For many I could not find a suitable description. . . . All were decorated by hand with characteristic Hopi designs; many were real showpieces, and of decided value. But what to do with a stock of that size."[6]

Schmedding paid Hubbell a few hundred dollars for the whole uncounted lot, assuming that he could dispose of it eventually at a profit. Tourists always took home a few souvenirs of pottery, Navajo rugs, and jewelry, but one particular visitor presented Schmedding with the opportunity to sell Hopi crafts to a new market. The vice president of B. Altman & Co., who had stopped at the post, ordered three thousand pieces to be shipped to the New York store on Fifth Avenue. From that sale, Schmedding developed a successful mail-order business, selling to exclusive shops and department stores, to corporations and to clubs, to hotels and to executives for their country homes.

The post itself and the trader's duties did not change. The

trader or his wife administered Argyrol solution to the granulated eyes of the residents to treat the prevalent trachoma. Indians flocked to the post at Christmas to receive bags of candy, peanuts, chewing gum, and packaged cookies, and, for the men, tobacco and cigarette papers. The lack of electricity, gas, telephone or telegraph, daily news, meat markets, laundries, or modern plumbing was "put up with and taken in stride. . . . For music [Schmedding and his wife] had a phonograph and a good-sized library of records embracing everything from popular songs to opera, and light dance music to symphonic composition. Sitting in front of a cheerful fire in the open fireplace [in the trader's house on the knoll] and listening to some fine records gave us a fair imitation of Carnegie Hall or the Metropolitan. And we could listen to those lovely airs without the deadly 'commercial' breaking in at the most enjoyable moment of the concert or opera!"[7]

A more dominant personality arrived in Keams Canyon in 1911: the new superintendent, Leo Crane. Finding himself responsible for a reservation of several autonomous pueblos spread out over three desolate mesas, he requested that Colonel Hugh L. Scott and an escort of the Twelfth Cavalry accompany him on an inspection tour. Both Scott and Crane observed and subsequently protested that four-fifths of the reservation was overrun by Navajos, who with their herds of sheep had forced the Hopis onto one-fifth of the land reserved for their use. Crane was appalled at the condition of the villages, particularly Oraibi and Hotevilla. Scott admonished Crane, "Young man! You have an empire to control. Either rule it or pack your trunk."[8]

Crane was concerned about sanitation and crowding at the school in Keams Canyon. Smallpox still threatened, measles and dysentery periodically ravaged the children, and tuberculosis afflicted not only the natives but also the white employees working with them. He succeeded in obtaining funds for the construction of a new training school and six permanent day schools to replace the temporary ones at the mesas. Children subsequently advanced from primary day school to the training school, and then to larger nonreservation schools in Albuquerque, Phoenix, and Riverside. During his tenure, a

23. Nampeyo at the Pendete Kiva. Original negative by J.R. Willis, ca. 1918. Contemporary print by Walter Haussamen. (Walter Haussamen Collection)

Painter-photographer Willis, who lived in Gallup from 1910–1920, photographed throughout the Southwest. Like many of his peers, he did not date his photographs. In this photo, the jar on the left with clown/kachina faces (Museum of Indian Arts and Culture, Museum of New Mexico, cat. #12079/12) was purchased by Edgar L. Hewett and given to the museum in 1924, but no purchase date was recorded. Considering Nampeyo's graying hair and the large "plump" jar she is shaping, I would date the photo about 1918.

hospital was built, wells were drilled to augment the water supply, and the roads were improved. His accomplishments were achieved despite "an unappreciative, often snarling Bureau, twenty-six hundred miles away, that understood little and corrected less, while it asked senseless questions that must be answered, made foolish decisions, and prepared for the field as many handicaps as distant ignorance and lack of sympathy could contrive."[9]

Concerned about published photographs sensationalizing the Snake Dance, Crane banned visitors from taking motion pictures for his descriptively clear reason:

> Members of the snake clan are peaceful natives, but they zealously enact their parts in the pageant every second year; and to see those fellows painted ferociously, garbed in savage dress, with snakes held in their mouths—I can conceive of no more terrible close-up than that of a Snake Priest, coming toward one with eyes glaring, cheeks and chin painted black, his mouth a huge white daube, and snakes, some of them with rattles feeling around his ears, through his hair, and about his face and nose. This would never do for general consumption.[10]

In 1917 one news service cameraman defied the rule and was chased through the desert so that his unauthorized motion picture could be confiscated. After dutifully reporting the incident to the commissioner of Indian affairs in Washington, Crane received the order that no photographs should be permitted thereafter, a ban continued by Hopi elders today.

In his 1917 report to the commissioner of Indian affairs, Crane recommended changing the name of the agency and reservation from the detested "Moqui" to "Hopi," which was preferred by the people themselves. No action was taken.

"Distant ignorance and lack of sympathy" was not confined to the Washington Bureau of Indian Affairs but permeated individual thinking in the Bureau of American Ethnology as well. When Jesse Walter Fewkes concluded his research in Hopi in the late 1890s, he shifted his attention to do field work in the West Indies, Mexico, Casa Grande in Arizona, Mesa Verde National Park in Colorado, and Navajo National Monument in Arizona. In 1918, he was appointed director of the bureau itself. Eventually, he returned to the subject of Hopi ceramics in a paper about design symbols painted on prehistoric Hopi pottery.[11] The only Hopi potter named in the paper was Nampeyo, whose reputation by the time of his writing had grown within the scientific community and among the public at large.

In the introduction to his essay, Fewkes stated that the renaissance of old Sikyatki patterns originated with Nampeyo, who had made pencil copies of designs on mortuary bowls when she visited the excavation of Sikyatki. "This modified Sikyatki ware [is] often sold by unscrupulous traders as ancient. . . . There is danger that in a few years some of Nampeo's imitations will be regarded as ancient Hopi ware."[12]

Later in the paper, in a discussion of the symbols of Hano clans, Fewkes reiterated that a sudden return from Tewan designs to the ancient Sikyatki style was due to the influence of Nampeyo, who, in 1895, began to "cleverly imitate" Sikyatki ware. However, in a footnote to his disparaging comments about the potter, he claimed partial credit for the revival himself:

> Much of the pottery offered for sale by Harvey and other dealers in Indian objects along the Santa Fe Railroad in Arizona and New Mexico is imitation prehistoric Hopi ware made by Nampeo. The origin of this transformation was due partly to the author, who in the year named [1895] was excavating the Sikyatki ruins and graves. Nampeo and her husband, Lesou, came to his camp, borrowed paper and pencil, and copied many of the ancient symbols found on the pottery vessels unearthed, and these she had reproduced on pottery of her own manufacture many times since that date.[13]

By the time of his writing, about twenty years after the excavation, more public recognition had been given to Nampeyo's reputation as a potter than to his personal discovery and excavation of Sikyatki ceramics. By reiterating his own interpretation of events, he again diverted attention from the nebulous origin of the revival style begun in the 1880s to his excavation of Sikyatki ware in 1895.[14]

Yet another published article distorted the Sikyatki story by adding a belated embellishment. The writer, Walter Hough, was not present at the site during the excavation, so his source of information remains unknown. However, the friendship between Hough, Fewkes, and another archaeologist, Edgar L. Hewett, who had encouraged potter Maria of San Ildefonso, is suggestive.

Edgar L. Hewett, a teacher from New Mexico, traveled to Washington about 1900 to meet the pioneer anthropologists in the Eastern establishment.[15] Befriended by those in the Bureau of American Ethnology and the National Museum—John Wesley Powell, William H. Holmes, and Jesse Walter Fewkes among others—Hewett retired from teaching in 1904 to pursue his avocation in archaeology. By 1907, when Hewett began his archaeological work in New Mexico, he had formed close relationships with many renowned in that field.

Hewett's interest lay in the ruins on the Pajarito Plateau above San Ildefonso Pueblo, and he hired men from the pueblo to do the manual labor. One of them, Julian Martinez, left his new wife, Maria, at home the first summer, but she accompanied Julian to camp the following year. When Hewett found petroglyphs in a cave on the plateau, he gave paper and pencil to Julian and asked him to copy the drawings. During the excavation, the crew found potsherds and polishing stones used by prehistoric potters, which they showed to Maria. Hewett asked her if she could copy the pottery in the old way with the old designs. She said she would try, but since she did not know how to draw, Julian would have to paint the designs.

During the following year at the pueblo, Maria and Julian worked at reproducing the pottery. When Hewett returned, he not only purchased several pieces that they had made but also ordered more to resell. Thus, Hewett was credited with the revival of an ancient pottery style made by a gifted potter whose husband worked for the archaeologist at the site.

It is unlikely that Walter Hough would have confused names, dates, and places of experiences exchanged informally among scientific peers. It is entirely possible that Fewkes appropriated Hewett's account for his own benefit. Whatever its basis, a brief article written in 1917 by Hough summarized the deterioration of pottery on the Hopi mesas, and then added:

It is to the credit of an Indian woman, a native of Hano named Nampeo, that the ancient potters' art of the Hopi has been revived. The manner of the happening is interesting. Nampeo's husband, Lesu, a Hopi, worked for Dr. Fewkes on the excavations of Sikyatki, and Nampeo often visited the scene of his labors.[16]

Hough failed to question why Fewkes himself had never reported that Lesso was one of his workers. In all of Fewkes's writings, Lesso was merely the husband who accompanied Nampeyo to the site to assist her in copying designs from the ancient ware.

Frederick Webb Hodge, who assisted Fewkes at the Sikyatki excavation in 1895, named seven of the ten Hopis hired as workmen: Wazhri, Pringtinia, Wupa, Hanakashi, Mungwe, Kopele, and "The Spaniard."[17] Had Lesso been one of the three unnamed workers, it seems unlikely that he would have been allowed to sit with his wife copying designs while others excavated, considering the slow pace at which the excavation proceeded.

Whatever the foundation or reason for Hough's erroneous revelation, Lesso's "employment" enhanced Fewkes's role in the revival of Hopi pottery, inevitably linking his name to Nampeyo's. The timing of the publication of Fewkes's essay and of Hough's short article was beneficial for Fewkes, for few would question the accuracy of reports of archaeological activities two decades earlier.

Diminishing Sight

"Thy eyes so dim."
—*Borg,* Nam-Pey-O

When the United States entered World War I in 1917, visitors virtually disappeared from the mesas.

> *There was hardly much people here. Once in a while.*
> *Maybe one party come in one whole year.* (1986)

Except for the continuing presence of sculptor Emry Kopta, trader Joseph Schmedding, superintendent Leo Crane, and a few government employees, the environment during the war years must have been reminiscent of old times on the mesas. There were no crowds with cameras, questioning scientists and reporters with their notebooks and pencils, or souvenir-hunting tourists. The kachinas arrived with the Soyal ceremony in winter and left with the Niman in summer, and the dances were witnessed only by those for whom they had inherent meaning.

In need of money to finance the war, the federal government expected Indian agents to sell a fair share of Liberty Bonds to the people under their jurisdictions. Crane explained the crisis to his charges, using the pictorial sections of the *New York Times* that depicted soldiers and battlefields, airplanes and submarines. The photographs astonished the residents of the barren mesas, but Crane faced a problem. The Hopis were inclined to hold onto their earnings, secreting their money in storage jars or holes in the walls of their homes, unlike the Navajos, who spent money in the trading posts and entrusted their savings to the agents. Crane surmised that if Tom Pavatea could be convinced to buy the bonds others would follow.

Prior to a meeting Crane had called of First Mesa residents, an agency employee approached Pavatea, challenging him to buy some bonds and offering to match him dollar for dollar. When the people gathered, Crane explained the country's involvement in a war and the need for guns, ammunition, clothing, blankets, medicine, and food. Pavatea produced a certificate of deposit for one thousand dollars with which to purchase bonds, and the agency employee matched the purchase. Another resident then pledged four hundred dollars and other Hopis followed with smaller sums. During five sales campaigns, Crane sold $11,600 in bonds to one hundred and thirty Hopis and Tewas, whose right thumbs were pressed to an ink pad and printed on the papers in place of signatures.

Another call from Washington invited the Indians to contribute curios to a bazaar to be held in the capital city, the proceeds from which would be used to finance a hospital unit. Doubtful of the response, Crane communicated the request to the mesas. Within a short time, his warehouse overflowed with hundreds of donations: jewelry, weavings, reed plaques and baskets, and pottery. "A tenderly whimsical thought," Crane wrote later. "The vision of some wounded lad finding relief through an old Hopi woman's moulding and baking clay figures, far from the hysteria of the cities, far from the guns and stench of war, but contributing the one thing she knew, while humming some chant, perhaps of ancient battles."[1]

Nampeyo surely contributed, but the value of her unsigned vessels among the others sent to Washington was unknown to many of the Easterners who purchased "curios" to support the war effort. When peace returned, some of the handcrafted items indigenous to the Southwest may have been discarded, as mementos often are, sold in rummage sales, or donated to museums, their provenance unknown.

During those quiet years on the mesa, the men still had their work in the fields and their kiva activities. What of the women who no longer had to grind corn or to make utilitar-

ian pottery, women who had made souvenirs and piki for white visitors? What of Nampeyo, who had traveled to distant places to demonstrate her skills, who had made vessels for collectors and for museums? Being a creative artist, she continued to shape her clay, perhaps in a manner to compensate for her diminishing eyesight. Documentation is lacking, but evidence enforces the belief that she began to make more tactile decorations and shapes. A photograph taken by Emry Kopta around 1920 is the earliest to show a jar with a corrugated neck; several other corrugated jars (Plate 13, for example) can be attributed to this period. Jars with square orifices, and large, graceful storage jars (Plate 14) may also have been shaped by her hands during this quiet, transitional time.

Twenty years had passed since Dr. Joshua Miller had treated Nampeyo's eyes, during which time her trachoma would have gone into remission, recurred, and eventually clouded her

24. Nampeyo with a corrugated jar. Emry Kopta, ca. 1920. (Museum of Northern Arizona. Photo #MS240–2–442)

Nampeyo looks older in this undated photo that may have been taken shortly before Kopta left Hopi in 1922. Because of diminished eyesight, Nampeyo was adding tactile decoration to her vessels during this period.

vision. Belatedly, two observers commented about Nampeyo's inability to see clearly by the 1920s. Three decades after visiting the potter during the summer of 1920, Neil M. Judd wrote that "Nampeyo was already nearly blind."[2] Nearly five decades after studying pueblo potters in 1924 and 1925, an elderly Ruth Bunzel stated that Nampeyo had been totally blind at the time,[3] although Bunzel did not mention Nampeyo's lack of sight or inability to paint in her scholarly text.[4]

Memories are frequently distorted by time and intervening events, but the most credible evidence of Nampeyo's diminished vision comes from artist Carl Oscar Borg in 1920. Swedish-born Borg arrived in Southern California in 1903 and later became the protégé of Phoebe Apperson Hearst. At her behest, the University of California and Bureau of American Ethnology commissioned him to paint and photograph the Hopi and Navajo Indians. Borg lived among the people on those reservations on frequent trips between 1916 and 1932, and among his subjects was Nampeyo. Inspired by the potter, he wrote a poem:

Nam-Pey-O

I see thy busy fingers mould the desert clay.
Where are thy models?
Thy eyes so dim—what inner vision do they see?
So I watch.
It seems to me that all around
Thy room are the silent workers of thy art—
The last ones of thy race.
What work in bits is strewn across
the desert waste is coming—one by one . . .
I seem to hear them speak in whispers low—

"NAM - PEY -O!"

"Fashion well and strong—thou last of our famous Guild . . . and paint the symbols of our faith . . . the Gods of Rain and Air!"[5]

Borg spoke of "eyes so dim" but mentions that she should "paint the symbols of our faith." Throughout Bunzel's text, Nampeyo's painting is described in the present tense. "At times her patterns are almost impressionistic in their economy."[6]

Commenting on three large storage jars made by Nampeyo, Bunzel stated, "The design in its elements and arrangement was different from every other Hopi design, and very much cruder."[7] Such descriptions would be consistent with a painter's inability to handle fine brushwork.

It is apparent that Nampeyo continued to paint through the war years and perhaps later, but with less refinement. At what time does an artist admit that painting is no longer possible? There can be no determinate point.

A war that changed the country, her diminished vision, and deterioration of tradition all within a short period of time profoundly altered the lives of Nampeyo and Lesso. By 1920, they had also lost both of their elder sons.

Following the war, a devastating influenza epidemic swept the country. Countless natives who perished on the mesas were buried by the Baptist missionaries, Joseph Schmedding, and anyone else who could assist in the depressing task. During the epidemic, Nampeyo's second son, William, was hired by Schmedding to haul freight between the trading post and the railroad at Holbrook. When a snowstorm engulfed him on one of the trips, he attempted to walk to Indian Wells for help, but his feet froze before he could find shelter. Gangrene set in and he died of blood poisoning. Kaloakuno had died of smallpox several years earlier.[8] By 1920, Nampeyo and Lesso were living alone in the old stone house at the top of the trail.

Despite the country's involvement in the war, arrogance and politics still dominated the government's administration of the reservation. In 1919, the Bureau of Indian Affairs transferred Superintendent Crane to New Mexico and appointed Robert E. L. Daniel as his replacement. During a visit to see the Snake Dance in Walpi, the painter Charles M. Russell described Daniel as "swellin' around in a Palm Beach suit and carryin' a cane."[9] Daniel attempted to prohibit the ceremonial dances and denigrated the artists, photographers, anthropologists, and those sympathetic to the Hopis, whom he considered social misfits who interfered with his authority.

Emry Kopta, living with Pavatea's family in Polacca, was anathema to the new superintendent, who expressed relief when the sculptor moved from the reservation in 1922. In both traditional Christian and Hopi ceremonies, Kopta married Anna Phelps, a teacher in the Phoenix Indian School, who had taught several of Nampeyo's grandchildren. Although he moved to Phoenix with Anna, he continued to return to the mesa to obtain clay from Nampeyo.[10] Daniel called the sculptor an itinerant artist who had been a disturbing element among the Hopi people, and he recommended (without success) that no visitors' permits be issued to artists and writers for periods longer than ninety days.

Daniel's most abhorrent act took place in 1920. Armed with revolvers and hickory buggy spokes, Daniel, agency employees, and policemen under his direction went to Hotevilla, gathered all residents—men, women, children, old and young alike—and forcefully threw them into sheep dip to cleanse them. The only offensive part of the activity, he complained, was the revolting vituperation of the women and obscene language of the English-speaking men.

Superintendent Daniel's continued arrogance reverberated among Indian sympathizers into a campaign to reform government policies. While emotions erupted nationally and mesa residents retreated in fear and hatred, a scandal within the federal government finally effected a change.

In 1923, after nine years of conscientious service at his trading post, Joseph Schmedding received a curt letter from Secretary of the Interior Albert B. Fall revoking his license as an Indian trader at Keams Canyon. The letter cited administrative reasons; in actuality, a wholesaler friend of Fall's in Gallup coveted the post. Only the president of the United States could have intervened in Schmedding's behalf, but Warren G. Harding was a personal friend of the secretary. Appealing to his own acquaintances, Schmedding obtained the support of senators, congressmen, and lawyers, while reporters already were probing more sensational charges against Fall.

The critical attention focused on Fall's activities revealed that the secretary had accepted a large bribe to lease the U.S. Naval Oil Reserve in Wyoming to private speculators who then sold the oil back to the navy at tremendous profit. The Teapot Dome Scandal led to Fall's indictment, conviction, and subsequent prison term in a federal penitentiary.

Although Schmedding succeeded in retaining his license, the strife, the bitterness, and the concern about the education of his growing children induced him to sell the post the following year. The new trader, Earl F. Halderman, took possession at the same time that public pressure forced the dismissal of Superintendent Robert E. L. Daniel.

Finally, in 1923, the name of the Moqui Agency in Keams Canyon was changed to the Hopi Agency, and in 1924 Congress passed a bill granting United States citizenship to Native Americans, giving them the privilege to vote and the obligations to perform compulsory military duty when called and to pay taxes on off-reservation revenues.

Alone

"He always go around everywhere she goes." (1982)

The aftermath of World War I effected a dramatic change in values throughout the nation, for the 1920s were a decade of growth and accelerating technology. Automobile production boomed, making it possible for families to explore the country on roads that were often unmarked and unpaved.

The Southwest had become known as an enchanted land toward which vacationers rattled in Model-T Fords, carrying spare parts and camping gear. The motorists wanted to see stereotypical Indians and to buy inexpensive souvenirs of their trip. Many native craftsmen and commercial traders were happy to accommodate the new consumers, but a few concerned citizens began to sponsor Indian fairs in which crafts judged for quality were sold directly to the public by native artists. Based on traditional intertribal gatherings at which Native Americans bartered with each other, the publicized events were held in or near towns that offered overnight accommodations, or at least some conveniences, to travelers. The Santa Fe Indian Market, first held in 1921, and the Gallup Ceremonial, begun in 1922, for example, attracted crowds of vacationing tourists who could find an array of crafts made and sold by pueblo and tribal craftsmen in native dress.

Hopis who were unable or unwilling to leave their mesa homes to participate in the multitribal festivals relied on the more adventurous travelers who followed Highway 66 paralleling the Santa Fe Railway across northern Arizona. At Holbrook they could turn north on old dirt wagon tracks that took them directly to Keams Canyon and, eleven miles farther, to Polacca.

Because of seasonal flurries of vacationers, the new trader, Earl Halderman, built an addition of several rooms next to Keam's old house on the knoll near the post, where he could accommodate a few visitors. Other travelers were permitted to stay in the day schools near the mesas during the summer months, but many set up camp around Polacca, where younger Hopi and Tewa generations were raising their families. Leaving their cars below, visitors hiked the trail to see the deteriorating villages where only elder generations remained.

The trail that had been widened in the early 1880s to allow wagons to be pulled to the top was again inadequate for modern-day "traffic." During the 1920s, a new road with a more gradual ascent for automobiles was blasted into the cliff below the Corn clan dwellings, destroying the Pendete Kiva that, again, was relocated by blasting near Nampeyo's house. The new road terminated in the middle village of Sichomovi, where visitors left their cars. Wandering among the stone dwellings, sightseers could walk to Walpi in one direction and to the plaza of Hano in the other, without knowing that the best potter on the mesa was molding her vessels at the top of a trail that had become obsolete.

When dances and ceremonies took place on the mesa, souvenirs and untraditional items that provided an expedient income for their makers were laid out on rugs around the plaza for sale. Even Nampeyo succumbed to the temptation to make pottery objects that would appeal to souvenir-collecting tourists. Isolated from other vendors, she made rain god figurines in the style of those made in Tesuque Pueblo north of Santa Fe, New Mexico. Where she had seen the popular Tesuque figures is unknown, but they were tactile and shaping them obviously appealed to her senses. Four sold by Tom Pavatea in 1922 are the best documented examples (Plate 23). A more unusual effigy exists in the collection of the Phoebe Hearst Museum of Anthropology, University of California, Berkeley, with "by Nampeyoh" penciled on the base.[1]

From about 1917 through the 1920s, the least recorded period of Nampeyo's life, her pottery-making went through widely divergent changes. A sudden termination of buyers during World War I followed by the arrival of souvenir-seeking tourists coincided with the final phase of trachoma from which there was no remission. Turning from elegant jars of large proportions and designs with confident brushwork to more tactile jars with corrugations and figurines for the tourist trade, Nampeyo attempted to compensate for her declining eyesight. By the mid–1920s, perhaps not seeing well enough even to make tactile shapes and designs, she returned to the vessels her hands could shape with familiarity. During the summers of 1924 and 1925, Ruth Bunzel found Nampeyo and her daughter making "no worthless trifles. She makes only dignified pieces in the best traditional style. Technically, her work is superior to that of any other Hopi potter."[2] The general mass of Hopi pottery Bunzel described as "utterly worthless,"[3] "abominable," and "lacking in distinction."[4]

In 1927 a collection of eighty-six pottery items was purchased at First Mesa by Professor and Mrs. Carey E. Melville.[5] During a tour of the country in their Model-T Ford, the family stayed three weeks with missionary friends at the Baptist Church in Polacca. Acquiescing to the wishes of their hosts not to attend traditional ceremonies on the mesa or to mingle with non-Baptist Hopis, the Melvilles bought their pottery either directly from potters associated with the church or from Tom Pavatea. Among their purchases were a small undecorated, red-slip canteen signed "Nampaya" and a fine seed jar with a migration pattern signed "Annie Nampeyo." The remainder of the Melvilles' collection included bowls, tulip-shaped vases, amorphous jars, souvenir ashtrays, and little cowboy hats and boots. They illustrate Bunzel's frequent use of the term "mediocrity" in her critical discussion of contemporary Hopi pottery in general.

When the Southwest became accessible to motoring tourists, the Fred Harvey Company introduced "Indian Detours" in Harvey cars. Based in Santa Fe, the first touring cars in 1926 took "dudes" to the neighboring Rio Grande pueblos. Later, overnight trips to the north and south were added to their destinations, and within three years Harvey cars were transporting vacationers into Navajo and Hopi country.

Tours to view the Hopi Snake Dance averaged sixty people, who roughed it in luxury Fred Harvey style. Trucks carried tents complete with cots, blankets, pillows, lanterns, and wash basins. Tables and chairs were set up to create portable outdoor dining halls. Beverages, foodstuffs, and cooking equipment crowded the makeshift Harvey kitchens. Female couriers told Hopi legends and explained the ritual of the Snake Dance to the excited tourists before they ascended to the tiny plaza in Walpi for the ceremony.

Although tour leaders emphasized scenery and ceremony in their talks, the participants were free to explore the mesa before beginning the long, hot return in the Harvey cars. Those who did not buy souvenirs from the local residents on the mesa or from traders Pavatea and Halderman found an adequate display of merchandise in gift shops in the Harvey hotels and restaurants.

The stock market crash in 1929 terminated the prosperous decade. Those who had speculated in credit-buying became instant paupers, but many people were not affected until aftershocks rippled through the economy in the early 1930s. By 1931, the Depression was pandemic. Dependent on travelers and commerce in Indian crafts, the Fred Harvey Company's empire disintegrated. Few people could afford to travel for pleasure, and the market for pueblo pottery and kachina dolls, for silver jewelry and basketry, for fine Navajo rugs and other weavings had collapsed. Herman Schweizer reluctantly acknowledged that Harvey gift shops could sell only inexpensive, modern souvenirs.

On the mesa clan houses continued to deteriorate, and the old ones who inhabited them endured recurring health problems from the lack of sanitary facilities. Like many others, Lesso suffered from dysentery. Aged, feeble, and severely weakened by the disease, Lesso contracted influenza, then pneumonia, and died on the morning of May 7, 1930. According to Hopi tradition, the oldest woman of Lesso's Cedarwood clan would have washed his hair and whispered a secret name in his ear, the name he would take into the next world. A mask of raw cotton with two holes for the eyes and one for the mouth would have been placed over his face and secured around the forehead with a cord to which feathers were attached. Lesso's uncles or other male relatives from his father's Horn clan carried his body wrapped in a blanket to the Christian cemetery below, where he was buried on the same day of his death.

He always go around everywhere she goes. (1982)

After fifty years of marriage and companionship, of raising children and grandchildren, of witnessing the deterioration of ancient customs, Nampeyo was left alone in the rooms that had sheltered succeeding generations of Tewas since their migration from New Mexico around 1702.

The numbers of tourists that ascended the mesa during the prosperous '20s diminished as they had during the war. Once more, the reservation was quiet. In an effort to continue selling their crafts, some families moved for the summer months to Highway 66, where they constructed temporary shelters alongside the road and set up tables to display their wares to passing motorists.

Mary-Russell Ferrell Colton, who with her husband, Dr. Harold Sellers Colton, founded the Museum of Northern Arizona in Flagstaff in 1928, observed the proliferation of inferior Hopi crafts with concern. She deplored the tendency of the natives to compromise their work and condemned the mass of cheap junk being sold by the Indians along the highways. She felt it to be essential that institutions and traders cooperate to encourage higher quality and renewed pride in indigenous crafts.

Encouraged by the success of numerous organized Indian fairs, Colton planned the first annual Hopi Craftsman Exhibition to be held at the Museum of Northern Arizona on the Fourth of July, 1930, when, it was hoped, there would be tourists on the road. She, Edmund Nequatewa, and another museum employee visited the mesas to explain the concept and its potential benefits to the craftsmen, many of whom agreed to participate. All items to be displayed were required to pass a jury, and ribbons and cash prizes were to be awarded in various categories. Colton encouraged the participants to identify their pieces with an individual mark, so that each could build a personal reputation. Within a few years, the rules for participation became more stringent, detailing what types of crafts the museum would show and explaining its criteria for judging quality.

Forty-nine vessels, all with identifying marks or signatures, were accepted in the ceramics category for the first exhibition, of which forty-six were sold to the attending public. Thirteen women from Hano participated, including Lucy Harvey, Sadie Adams, Irene Gilbert, Grace Chapella, Nampeyo, and "Mrs. Healing." Nampeyo's single entry, a decorated olla, sold for two dollars. Annie's contributions—two bowls, one olla, one seed jar, and one globose jar—were priced from 50 cents to $1.50.

Nampeyo did not participate in the second exhibition in 1931, but fifteen other Hano women, including Paqua Naha, submitted their work. Annie entered two pieces: a large decorated jar priced at $7.00, the most expensive entry in the pottery category, and a small jar priced at $1.50. No entries were submitted by Nampeyo or her family in 1932, the year in which Colton continued encouraging higher quality of workmanship: "Potters! Use care and see that your *designs do not rub off*. We cannot accept pottery with designs that rub off."[6]

The aging Nampeyo entered three pieces in 1934, and vessels made by Nampeyo and painted by Fannie (Plate 24) were entered in 1934, 1935, and 1936. The requirement to identify the maker on each piece explains those few extant vessels bearing the name "Nampeyo" printed for her by a family member.

As the exhibit drew larger crowds every year, the museum initiated demonstrations by various craftsmen. Poli of Sichomovi fired pottery in 1935, from the building of a fire at 9 A.M. to the removal of fired pots from the ashes at 4:25 P.M. Of six smaller pieces and three larger ones, only two had fired perfectly, the others having broken or flaked on the surface. Mesa women watching the process nodded and confirmed that they too had had difficulty in firing their pottery on First Mesa that spring. They blamed it on witches.

You have to understand a superstition. Annie told me that they never fired here [on the mesa]. Lesso and her would take their pottery and go away from the mesa to fire. They think if you fire here the clouds won't come. These days when they have a dance, some of them tell you not to fire the pottery 'cause, when the clouds come up, they go away if you raise the smoke. (1986)

The Museum of Northern Arizona's Hopi Craftsman Exhibition has continued annually with great success, skipping only the World War II years of 1943 to 1946. It has been criticized for setting restrictive standards and stimulating commercialism, but it has fulfilled Colton's original purpose of encouraging improved craftmanship and establishing individual reputations for the artisans.

During the museum's early efforts to renew pride in Hopi craftsmen, Congress adopted the Wheeler Howard Act of 1934. Known as the Indian Reorganization Act, it terminated attempts to break up native landholdings and provided loans for schooling, medical service, soil conservation, and the development of arts and crafts. These and other benefits were dependent upon a tribe's acceptance by popular vote of self-government as proposed by the act. Explaining the advantages of creating a tribal constitution and a council with singular tribal authority to the several autonomous Hopi pueblos, each made up of separate clans, met with general opposition. The concept of one central political body was contrary to their centuries-old tradition. On October 24, 1936, fewer than 20 percent of the Hopi residents exercised their right to vote. Only those progressives who had moved into New Oraibi (Kykotsmovi), residents of Walpi, and the Tewas of Hano supported the change. They constituted less than 15 percent of the adult population, but their votes were sufficient to adopt the reorganization provisions for the entire Hopi Reservation. The Navajo Reservation rejected the act outright.

The elders who opposed the Wheeler Howard Act feared that any federal proposal would lead to further loss of their land. Their fear was confirmed when the Hopi and Navajo reservations were divided into grazing districts in 1943. The Bureau of Indian Affairs administered District Six, which included only the immediate area of the Hopi pueblos, implementing severe stock reductions to improve grazing. The action imposed an immediate hardship on the Hopis. The remainder of the Hopi Reservation was assigned to Navajo agencies to administer. The Hopi land base by then had shrunk to a fraction of the area supposedly provided for their use in 1882.

"Democracy" on the reservation was intended to enable the federal government to deal with one representative of several disparate villages and, conversely, to allow the people to speak to the government with one voice. In reality, the plan has not been an unqualified success, for it could not heal the dissension between traditional and progressive elements among the Hopis, nor did it stop Navajo encroachment onto Hopi lands.

Death

"Where the church-goers are buried." (1986)

E.A. Burbank, who had drawn "redheads" of the Navajos and Hopis during the early 1900s, and Sarah Abbott, the Baptist missionary living in Polacca when Burbank and Jo Mora rented Nampeyo's government house, continued to correspond after the artist had left the reservation. In 1940, Miss Abbott visited Burbank in his home in San Francisco and advised him not to return to Hopi. "Such a change had taken place," she told him. "[They are] a different people from what they were forty years ago. Their homes modernized, radios, automobiles, and some of them going places in air machines. One of them had a large up-to-date store. Fine highways to the different mesas, like all over California, all dressed in modern civilian clothes. And all speaking good English. And but very few of the old Indians living."[1]

Miss Abbott, who had spent her younger years striving to convert the people to Christianity and to more "civilized" ways, should not have been surprised that "a change had taken place." But her critical reporting of modernization in Hopi lives was as excessive as her abhorrence of Hopi tradition had been when she was a young missionary.

Younger generations of Hopis and Tewas who had moved into the once-empty government houses spread out over the hillocks of Polacca still lived without electricity and running water. Kerosene lamps illuminated the houses at night, and a few spigots had been placed outside in the village where the women filled buckets with water for their families. During windstorms, blowing sands obstructed the only dirt road linking the mesas and the outside world. True, residents dressed in "civilian" clothes, originally imposed by schools and the missionaries themselves, but English was still a second language in their lives.

Material change was not that significant, but the routine of their lives had been altered considerably. The young parents who sent their children to the Polacca Day School (at that time from kindergarten through high school, around which the present day school has grown) themselves had received compulsory education. They had learned how to read and to write, and many daughters who had been raised in the lower village no longer learned, nor did they want to learn, how to make pottery from the old sajas. Nor did the men have an opportunity to support their growing families. They had been "Americanized" on an isolated reservation, and in the 1930s, the nation outside was in the throes of a great depression.

On the mesa, the stone dwellings continued to deteriorate as a result of partial abandonment and neglect.[2] The men did not spin or weave clothing except for ceremonial robes and an occasional sash to trade or to sell. They still planted corn and raised some livestock, but they did not hunt rabbits or deer as before. Much of their time was spent in the kivas, socializing with their peers.

Women no longer ground corn every morning or made utilitarian pottery, but the old potters were encouraged by Mary-Russell Ferrell Colton to renew their skills to make vessels for the Hopi Craftsman Fair. They may have been skeptical at laboring for the prospect of selling a few pots each July. Initially, bowls outnumbered small jars among the entries, but sales at the fair encouraged better production. Colton's timely concept materialized when trading posts burgeoned with clay vessels. Pavatea traded more staples for lambs and livestock for shipment outside the reservation than he traded for crafts. No one was buying.

Beneath the surface of "modern" daily lives, friction still existed between families and among clans. Bunzel recorded that "one of the best potters of Hano" (whom she did not name) was not familiar with the craft of other women because her work at the Polacca Day School "coupled with the usual snobbishness of members of aristocratic pueblo families" kept her from visiting a great deal in the village.[3] But a semblance of tradition continued as it had for past generations. During ceremonies, the mesa returned to life, reminiscent of the old times; families ascended to their clan houses for festivities and Nampeyo's extended family filled the Corn clan house. There were no chairs, just a banco around the perimeter of the room where they sat, and Nampeyo fed them all. She would tell them that the dances had changed, that, as the old ones died, knowledge of the rituals was being lost.

Except for those brief periods of festivity, however, Nampeyo lived alone, with restricted vision, a tiny stooped figure with the gnarled hands characteristic of her trade. As the old saja of her family, she cared for the well-being of her children and grandchildren, and Tom Pavatea always accepted her vessels in exchange for the groceries she needed to feed them. Making her way down the road to one of her families, she would ask, "Who wants to help me?" One or another of the children would carry a bucket of clay or her provisions to her house, where the child was rewarded with candy.

Nampeyo continued to work the clay and to shape her vessels, even though she could not see well enough to paint them. Sometimes Annie or occasionally Fannie would paint the designs, but if her daughters were not available, she would carry the vessel to Lena Charlie, who lived on the plaza, or perhaps to others. At the time, it was unimportant. "She was just an Indian who made pretty pots. They didn't appreciate her. She was nobody."[4]

> People thought she was silly still making pottery. But she was an artist and artists don't stop working. (1995)

Annie's eldest daughter, Rachel, sometimes fired her grandmother's pots outside her house in Polacca. Other times, Nampeyo took the vessels to Sand Hill ranch.

> When I was a little girl, she fired her pottery at the ranch because there was plenty of dung there. My grandfather [Willie Healing] would send a wagon and horses for her

and she would load her pots in it and fire them at the
ranch. We had lots of fun with that wagon. (1990)

When Nampeyo's son, Wesley, married a second time to
another Pima woman, he moved back to Polacca with Cecilia.
No house was available to them, however, because property
passed from Hopi or Tewa mother to daughter. Nampeyo gave
them permission to move into her government house in the
village below, while she remained on the mesa, isolated from
the plaza and casual visitors. In order to have a more visible
location for showing her pottery, Nampeyo asked Wesley to
build a wooden stand at the base of the road leading to the
top. When tourists came to watch the ceremonies, he helped
her down the hill with the pottery that she offered for sale.

My great grandmother had a buckskin bag with a draw-
string where she kept the coins, silver dollars. My grandfa-
ther or someone in the family helped her make change.
(1990)

It was there at her stand that a much younger Tewa potter
from Santa Clara Pueblo met the older one whose work she
admired. Margaret Tafoya had traveled to Hopi in August of
1937 with her son and instantly recognized the pots—*"big*
pots"—as the work of Nampeyo. "We were sisters, Corn clan,"
so the two "sisters," Tafoya about forty years younger than
Nampeyo, discussed their pottery. Raising her hand just so
high above the ground, the diminutive Margaret Tafoya remembered, "Oh, she was tiny!"[5]

Nampeyo had inspired many potters whom she never met,
and her place in history was already recognized by students,
professors, and others affiliated with the arts and sciences,
many of whom sought her out. If she was not at her stand by
the road, they knew they would find her at home on the mesa.
Passing through the plaza, they could pause at an open door
of a sparsely furnished room where one of the old residents
sold pop and snacks. With their refreshments, they continued
past the kiva and around behind the Tobacco clan dwellings,
knowing that Nampeyo would be there. Graciously, as she
had for photographers at the turn of the century, she would
pose for photographs and shape a pot while her visitors

25. An elderly Nampeyo. Tad Nichols, 1935. (Tad Nichols Collection)
   On a field trip as a student, Nichols photographed the potter. The old
lady was still shaping vessels that were painted by others in 1939, three
years before her death.

watched.[6] Her hands were still working the clay in 1939, three years before her death, when Douglas Douma wrote to a friend that Nampeyo "is very old now, but she still make potteries."[7]

She just stayed at her house up on top here. You might say she was taking care of herself. (1986)

Family stories differ about the circumstances of Nampeyo's injury shortly before her death. They agree, however, that she was walking the dirt road between her house and the village below when she fell and hurt her leg. Men were called to take her back to her house, but after several days of not feeling well, she was moved to her house below in which Wesley and Cecilia lived.[8] On July 20, 1942, after Cecilia had bathed her, Nampeyo fell asleep and died that evening. After her hair was washed and her body wrapped in the white robe saved from her wedding day, she was buried that night by male members of her father's clan in the Christian cemetery where Lesso lay. Not a formal area of measured plots, the cemetery covers a rocky saddle on a hill at the base of the mesa, in which the graves were dug where space could be found.

Where the church-goers are buried. Baptist, I guess. For members, but everybody else was being buried there till it got kind of full. They put a fence around it then and started using the hill. (1986)

Small rocks ringed each grave, some with a name scratched into a stone. When there was no more space, another graveyard was designated, leaving the old Christian cemetery to return to its natural state, with an overgrowth of grasses and shrubby plants, exposed to the sun and the wind and the snow.

Frederick Webb Hodge, then director of the Southwest Museum in Los Angeles, acknowledged Nampeyo's death two months later in a brief notice in the September 1942 issue of the museum's publication, *The Masterkey:*

DEATH OF NAMPEYO

Nampeyo, most renowned of Pueblo Indian potters, whose beautiful vessels have found their way by thousands to remote corners, passed away on July 20. Although often regarded as a Hopi because she was born and lived all of her life in one of the pueblos of Hopiland, Arizona, she was really a Tewa of Hano village on the East Mesa. Nampeyo first became known to the outside world after making several visits in 1895 to the camp of Dr. J. Walter Fewkes of the Bureau of American Ethnology, then engaged in excavating the ruins of Sikyatki, an ancient Hopi pueblo. With deft fingers she copied designs from the pottery vessels there uncovered, which she adapted to her own esthetic use for years afterward. Fortunately her ceramic art will be carried on by her three daughters, who were instructed in the craft by their mother. Nampeyo was about 75 years of age at the time of her death.[9]

The following issue of *The Masterkey* corrected the age previously attributed by Hodge. Based on the photograph of Nampeyo taken by William Henry Jackson in 1875, the correction estimated her age at death at about eighty-two.[10]

In subsequent correspondence between Dr. M.W. Stirling of the Smithsonian Institution and Dr. Harold S. Colton of the Museum of Northern Arizona, they agreed that "her passing deserves a little more than a mere notice."[11] Colton then sent Edmund Nequatewa to First Mesa to gather information for a more lengthy tribute, which was published under Nequatewa's byline, entitled "Nampeyo, Famous Hopi Potter."[12] The informal article contained numerous errors (see Appendix A); nevertheless, it became the unquestioned source of biographical information about the potter.

When Nampeyo integrated the forms and designs of ancient potters into a contemporary style of Hopi ceramics, utilitarian vessels made by women potters evolved into an art form, known during Nampeyo's lifetime only as Hopi Revival pottery. At the time of her death in 1942, the importance of her legacy was not realized by either her family or by the general public, for she died a traditional Tewa in a modern era, the "last of our famous Guild."[13] World War II had galvanized the country in war effort again, and in its aftermath decorated clay vessels gathered dust on trading post shelves. During the 1950s and 1960s, traders "couldn't give them away."[14] A decade later, Native American crafts became collectibles, material investments that created a new, enviable market for artisans. Succeeding generations of Nampeyo's descendants have adopted the name that Nampeyo could neither read nor write to fire on the bottoms of their contemporary clay pots. Collectors looking back to the inception of the common style have paid posthumous recognition to Nampeyo's talent, and an active market for her unsigned vessels, many without provenance, prevails.

In 1986, Nampeyo was elected to the Arizona Women's Hall of Fame. The monograph published by the Arizona Historical Society on that occasion began: "She's known among collectors of fine Hopi pottery simply as 'the old lady.' Superior craftsmanship is her trademark." The essay concluded: "Her art, inspired from centuries past, will be displayed and admired for centuries to come."[15]

The biographical summary, however, perpetuated the ubiquitous errors about the potter that no longer warrant repetition. Nampeyo herself could not clarify events in her life. She spoke no English; she left no words. Placing her in the context of Hopi history amid her own people and those outsiders who benefited from her talent and reputation, we find a tiny woman, an exceptional potter, a compulsive artist, who is a giant in the history of Hopi ceramics.

Part II.
Her Pottery

*They say the clay remembers
the hands that made it.*
  —*Byrd Baylor,* When Clay Sings

Plate 1.
Bowl made by Nampeyo.
Period 1, 1896. 8¼'' dia.
(National Museum of
Natural History, Smith-
sonian Institution, cat.
#158,176)

When Walter Hough,
curator of anthropology,
National Museum, visited
the Moqui Reservation in
1896, he made a collection
of seven bowls made by
Nampeyo. They are the
earliest documented
vessels made by the potter.

Plate 2.
Canteen made by Nam-
peyo. Period 1, pre-1900.
11¼'' high. (Arizona State
Museum, cat. #4099)

Before his death in
1901, Dr. Joshua Miller
spent summers on the
Moqui Reservation
ministering to the resi-
dents. Nampeyo gave this
canteen to the doctor for
treating her eyes, presumably for the prevalent
trachoma that diminished
her sight by the 1920s.

Plate 3.

Bowl made by Nampeyo.
Period 2, 1901. 3″ × 9¾″ dia.
(Middle American Research
Institute, Tulane University,
cat. #41-151)

Archaeologist George H.
Pepper attended the Snake
Dance in Walpi in 1901, at
which time he made a collection of twenty-two vessels
from Nampeyo, nineteen of
which remain in the collection. This bowl shows the
strong painting and typical
shape of Nampeyo's hand.

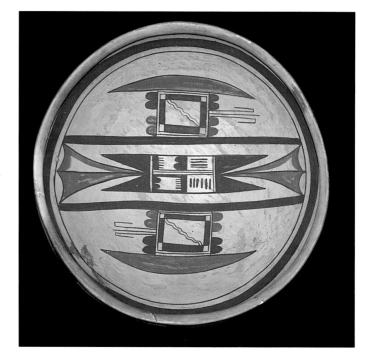

Plate 4.

Bowl made by Annie. Period
2, 1901. 2½″ × 9¼″ dia.
(Middle American Research
Institute, Tulane University,
cat. #41-156)

Several vessels attributed
to Nampeyo in the George H.
Pepper collection were made
by Annie. Her bowls were
more shallow and angular
(Figure 4) than Nampeyo's
bowls (Figure 3), and many
were painted with black or
black-and-white designs on a
red slip. The design in this
bowl, similar to those in two
red bowls in Vroman's 1901
photographs (Photographs 13
and 14), contains large black
areas with a paucity of line
work. The abstract concept of
two birds at a trumpet-
shaped flower was, I believe,
one of Annie's designs.

Plate 5.

Jar made by Nampeyo. Period 2, 1903. 4¾" × 10" dia. (Couse Family Collection)

Anxious to see the Snake Dance, artist E.I. Couse took his family to Walpi, where they stayed for six weeks. While her husband painted in villages on the three mesas, his wife, Virginia, and their son, Kibbey, frequently visited Nampeyo to watch her work. When the family returned to Taos, they carried with them this jar made by the potter.

Plate 6.

Bowl made by Nampeyo. Period 2, ca. 1905. 3½" × 10 ⅛" dia. (Denver Art Museum, cat. #1935.414)

The design in this bowl collected by Reverend Charles Winfred Douglas illustrates Nampeyo's innovative use of elements of the migration design (Figures D and E). A bowl with similar design (Hood Museum of Art, Dartmouth College, cat. #46-17-1011) collected by Frank and Clara Churchill (1904–1907) is signed "Numpayo" in a rectangle on the exterior below the rim. The catalog card notes that the signature appears to have been added after firing, no doubt by someone other than the potter.

Plate 7.

Jar made by Nampeyo. Period 2, ca. 1904-1910. 7″ × 15¾″ dia. (Museum of Indian Arts and Culture, Museum of New Mexico, cat. #18838/12)

Although the catalog card dates this jar from 1913-1915, the rectangular element with diagonal and frets within the eagle tail design was incorporated into many designs by the potter during the first few years of the 1900s.

Plate 8.

Storage jar attributed to Nampeyo. Date unknown. 11½″ × 12½″ dia. (Museum of Indian Arts and Culture, Museum of New Mexico, cat. #7721/12)

Nampeyo painted variations of the spider design in bowls and on jars most frequently during the first decade of the century.

Plate 9.
Jar made by Nampeyo.
Period 3, 1912. 9″ × 12″
dia. (Gilcrease Museum,
cat. #5437.4396)

Nampeyo painted this
stylized kachina design for
a short period, about
1912–1915, frequently
alternated with a circle
motif as seen on this
vessel. Her bold brush-
work contrasts with
Annie's painting of the
same design (Plate 10).
Both vessels were collected
by artist William R. Leigh.

Plate 10.
Jar made by Annie. Period
3, 1912. 5½″ × 9¼″ dia.
(Gilcrease Museum, cat.
#5437.4420)

"Made by the daughter
of Nam-pa-ya-Tawa. 1st
Mesa, Ariz. 1912″ is
marked on the bottom of
this red-slip jar. Artist
William R. Leigh not only
painted several portraits of
Annie but was the first to
attribute vessels to her.
Annie's more delicate
interpretation of a stylized
kachina design can be
contrasted with her mother's
strong painting of the same
design (Plate 9).

Plate 11.

Jar made by Nampeyo. Late Period 3, date unknown. 11″ × 20″ dia. (Arizona State Museum, Tucson, cat. #E-792)

Photographs do not capture the magnificence of this large jar painted with five batwing designs between two black framing lines. "Nampeyo" and "M 25.00" are written on the side of the vessel near the base.

Plate 12.

Jar attributed to Nampeyo. Date unknown. 8″ × 15″ dia. (School of American Research, cat. # 1418)

No figurative designs appear in dated photographs or documented collections of Nampeyo's work. This jar, the jar with clown/kachina faces in Photograph 23, and another jar painted with two maidens alternated with two abstract circle motifs (School of American Research, cat. #1645) bear a similarity of shape. Nampeyo painted circle motifs about 1912 to 1915, and I believe that she painted figurative designs and made the large "plump" shapes between 1915 and 1918.

Plate 13.

Jar made by Nampeyo. Early Period 4, date unknown. 5½″ × 9¾″ dia. (Arizona State Museum, Tucson, cat. #E-2273)

The names "J.R. Willis" and "Nampeyo" are written on the bottom of this jar. I believe that Willis took the photograph of Nampeyo working at the Pendete Kiva (Photograph 23) about 1918, when she began adding corrugations to her jars. As her eyesight diminished, the potter expressed her creativity with tactile forms.

Plate 14.

Storage jar attributed to Nampeyo. Date unknown. 13¾″ × 19¾″ dia. (Arizona State Museum, Tucson, cat. #GP-52543)

There are two magnificent, undocumented storage jars in this collection: 1. The catalog card for this one reads only, "Polychrome jar, Hopi. Square top, made by Nampeyo"; 2. A jar with round orifice of larger dimensions that was purchased from Fred Harvey's Commercial Hotel, Holbrook, in 1928 is also attributed to Nampeyo. I have found no evidence to date such jars, but I believe that they were made about 1920.

Plate 15.

Jar attributed to Nampeyo. Period 4, date unknown. 4¼″ × 8½″ dia. (Private collection)

This jar needs no documentation to identify its maker. Despite failing eyesight, Nampeyo's sense of whimsy remained intact as she pinched corrugations and pushed out bulges to resemble the corn of her clan. The fret design around the neck is not carefully painted, indicating her diminishing eyesight; the panel design was probably painted by another member of the family.

Plate 16.

Jar made by Nampeyo and painted by Annie. Period 5, ca. 1930s. 7⅞″ × 17⅞″ dia. (Museum of Indian Arts and Culture, Museum of New Mexico, cat. #18902/12)

During the last years of her life, Nampeyo again made the large-diameter, Sikyatki-shaped jars that earned her reputation at the turn of the century. The catalog card states that this one, collected and donated to the museum by Edgar L. Hewett, was "One of Nampeo's last pieces."

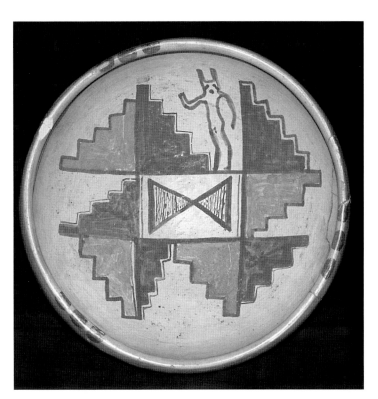

Plate 17.

Bowl made by Nampeyo. Period 2, 1901. $3^{1}/_{8}'' \times 9''$ dia. Red-and-black design on buff. (Middle American Research Institute, Tulane University, cat. #41-155)

The catalog card for this bowl collected by George H. Pepper describes the design as a "cloud decoration inside with human figure." Whether Nampeyo thought "human figure" or "spirit" is unknown, but the element adds a whimsical element to the design.

Plate 18.

Seed jar made by Annie. Period 2, date unknown 3" × 8¼" dia. (Mesa Verde National Park Museum, cat. #MEVE2615)

This seed jar attributed to Nampeyo is an early century jar made by Annie. Its shape is shallow and angular, and the red slip with black-and-white design is typical of Annie's work. The design lacks cohesion and the strong pattern of Nampeyo's authoritative hand. Similar seed jars are in the Pepper collection, Middle American Research Institute, Tulane University.

Plate 19.

Jar made by Nampeyo. Period 2, date unknown. 4½″ × 9½″ dia. Black-and-red design on cream slip. (Collection of Ernest and Virginia Leavitt)

Though slightly worn, the painting on this jar illustrates Nampeyo's enjoyment of improvising elements of designs into a cohesive pattern. She rarely painted a complete migration design. The "wingtips" frequently became the starting points of scrolls and other spontaneous shapes. Here, a clown face peers out from the band that flows into a rectangle with diagonals and extending frets, characteristic of work made in the early century.

Plate 20.

Bowl made by Nampeyo. Period 2, 1904. 9³/₈″ dia. Black-and-white pattern on red. (Ethnographic Museum, University of Oslo, Norway, cat. #13, 610-119)

Ole Solberg made a collection of eleven vessels from Nampeyo, eight of which were bowls with strong interior design. Three, including this bowl, were painted with random bands against an intricate "tweed" background.

Plate 21.

Jar made by Nampeyo. Period 2, 1904. 8″ × 16″ dia. Black-and-red design on buff. (Mesa Verde National Park Museum, cat. #MEVE3767)

Collected and donated to the museum by Mary Colter, Fred Harvey Company's architect and designer, this jar illustrates Nampeyo's mastery of placing five designs around the exterior of a vessel. The repeated double unit, more delicate than her bolder designs, is suggestive of a moth or butterfly and extended feathers.

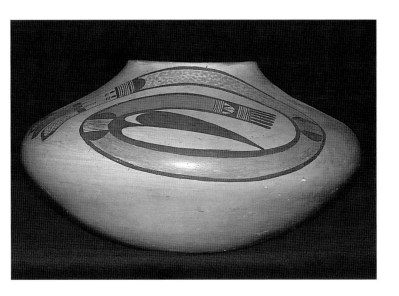

Plate 22.

Jar made by Nampeyo. Period 3, 1915. 7″× 12¾″ dia. Black-and-red design on tan slip. (School of American Research, Santa Fe, cat. #3011)

Nampeyo painted the abstract circle motif alone or alternated it with the stylized kachina design (Plate 9) during a very short period from about 1912 to 1915. This jar remained in the family of donor C. Phelps Dodge for over fifty years.

Plate 23.
Rain gods. Period 4, 1922. Approx. 12″ high. (Private collection. Photo by Gary N. Meek, M.D.)

Four "Nampayos Rain God @ 2.00 8.00" were purchased from Tom Pavatea's trading post in Polacca on April 12, 1922, by the present owner's grandfather. Not traditional Hopi craft, they were copies of effigies made at Tesuque Pueblo in New Mexico.

Plate 24.
Pitcher made by Nampeyo and painted presumably by Fannie. Period 5, ca. 1930s. 7¾″ long. Black-and-red design on buff. (Heard Museum, cat. #NA-SW-Ho-A7-98)

The bottom of the pitcher is signed with Nampeyo's name and another partially illegible name, presumably Fannie's. Late vessels printed with both Nampeyo's and one of her daughter's names may have been exhibited in the Museum of Northern Arizona's annual Hopi Craftsman Exhibition.

Stylistic Analysis of Vessels

During the nineteenth century, museums sent representatives into the Southwest to make massive collections of artifacts from the sites of prehistoric cultures and from the contemporary descendants of those cultures. Their purpose was not only to make impressive collections for their museums but to secure the thousands of pieces obtained for future study.

Archaeology was not yet a science, and only superficial information about unearthed objects was recorded at ancient ruins. The choice of areas to be excavated was left largely to the discretion of the directors of the expeditions, who dug at will before Indians realized that they could control their own lands. In the early twentieth century, Hopi elders closed their reservation to further digging, so that current analyses of prehistoric Hopi pottery must be made from pottery that was collected at random during the last century and documented by incomplete descriptive data.[1]

From 1879 through the decade of the 1880s, aggressive collecting of material culture from residents living on the three Hopi mesas produced an unexpected deviation in the style of pottery being made at that time. Realizing that heirloom pottery was more valued than the vessels they themselves were making, women began to replicate prehistoric pottery for barter with the acquisitive museum representatives. When museum collections burgeoned and extensive acquisitions ended, Nampeyo continued to integrate ancient shapes and designs into a personal, contemporary style that was known simply as Hopi Revival pottery during her lifetime.

In 1937, in an effort to coordinate studies of Hopi ceramics, Harold Colton and Lyndon Hargrave compiled the *Handbook of Northern Arizona Pottery Wares,* in which they proposed rules for the naming of newly recognized but hitherto unclassified pottery types. A new classification, they said, should be a geographic name followed by a descriptive term (such as Jeddito Black-on-yellow or Sikyatki Polychrome) and sufficiently clear so that it does not conflict with any other type.

Continuing his own research, Colton subsequently classified several previously unnamed Hopi pottery types and their variations. In a paper published in 1956, *Pottery Types of the Southwest,* he designated and described new classifications for Polacca Polychrome, Walpi Polychrome, Sichomovi Red Ware and Sichomovi Polychrome, and Hano Polychrome. He described Hano Polychrome as similar to the prehistoric Sikyatki Polychrome and attributed its origin to Nampeyo.

In recent years, however, the classification Hano Polychrome has sometimes been used to describe only unslipped vessels ("floated" surface, the coiled vessel being polished directly with a polishing stone). When thus used, the term Sikyatki Revival has referred to slipped vessels (a light "slip" of clay brushed over the surface, allowed to dry, and then polished). These more restrictive terms are not universally accepted, and they have confused Colton's original classification. Nampeyo made both slipped and unslipped vessels, but the identifying term Sikyatki Revival has been used frequently and erroneously to describe all pottery made in the style of Nampeyo. Perhaps it sounds more poetic, but it is inaccurate, for shapes and designs borrowed from Sikyatki ware constituted only one of many prehistoric periods incorporated by the potter. Even more mistakenly, the term gives credence to the myth that the style originated with the excavation of Sikyatki by Jesse Walter Fewkes in 1895. I have therefore chosen to use the designation Hano Polychrome, assigned by

Harold Colton, for it follows conventional rules for naming pottery types: It cites the geographic location of origin followed by a descriptive term and is sufficiently clear, not conflicting with any other type.

During the 1890s and early part of this century, Nampeyo was acknowledged to be the best pottery maker on First Mesa, the only one identified by name by outside observers. It is not known, therefore, how many other potters were making "commercial" as opposed to utilitarian vessels until the late 1920s, when potters were encouraged to identify their work with a mark or signature.

Nampeyo did not work with potters outside her family, so she did not consciously influence the work of others. Because she was so dexterous and productive, she unwittingly became the acknowledged leader of the revival style. It is important, however, not to attribute alien personality traits to this quiet, traditional Tewa woman. Nampeyo did not know ambition or practice deceit by using ancient pottery shapes and designs. She had an exceptional talent and received an inherent satisfaction in making pottery.

Annie was Nampeyo's silent but visible partner. She had inherited her mother's quiet temperament, and the two worked side by side, as evidenced in many photographs and descriptions by early writers. At the turn of the century, when Annie was not yet twenty years old, she was making and painting her own vessels, smaller and decorated with more simplistic designs than her mother's large, confident pieces. The earliest vessels I have found directly attributed to Annie, however, were collected in 1912 by William R. Leigh,[2] by which time they could have been mistaken for Nampeyo's work.

Where are all the vessels that Annie made prior to that date? Nampeyo was not aware that she would become renowned in the history of Hopi ceramics. She could not have understood the concept of a museum in which her pottery would be exhibited nor could she have comprehended the increasing value of her work. At the turn of the century, she was making pots that she set outside her house on a rug for visitors to buy, and when her eldest daughter began potting too, Nampeyo set Annie's out on the rug along with her own.

When visitors purchased the work of either, the name "Nampeyo" was attributed to the vessel.

The collection of vessels purchased by George H. Pepper from Nampeyo in 1901 exemplifies this practice.[3] Several bowls are of typical, inward-rolled rim shape (Figure 3) with bold interior polychrome designs (Plate 3) including one with a whimsical figure emanating from the design (Plate 17). Other bowls (Plate 4) and several small seed jars with truncated necks are more shallow and angular in profile (Figure 4) and painted with more simplistic designs uncharacteristic of Nampeyo's strong, free style. A red-slip seed jar with black-and-white design and truncated neck (Plate 18) in the Mesa Verde National Park Museum is similar to those collected by Pepper and is also attributed to Nampeyo.

After questioning where Annie's vessels might be and then comparing vessels in collections, I found that Annie's typical work was recognizable: She liked to paint black and black-and-white designs on red slip. Her early designs were more timid and generally lacked cohesion. Her early bowl designs incorporated large black elements with a paucity of linework. Her early shapes were more shallow and more angular than her mother's. As her work matured, it had a more delicate, horizontal feeling to it, like slanted penmanship. She was the first to repeatedly paint migration designs, her signature dots identifiable at the end of the "wingtips" (Plate 16).

Annie was a fine technical potter, but her designs were not as spontaneous as her mother's nor did she improvise with varying design elements. She was not a prolific potter and, after the 1930s, suffered from arthritis, which curtailed her pottery-making. Certainly she did not always paint black or black-and-white designs on red-slipped vessels. They happen to be the most easily recognizable, such as those in the Pepper collection at Tulane University and the Mesa Verde Museum. More comparison and analysis may make it possible to identify other vessels that Annie made before she began signing her work in the late 1920s. That many were attributed to Nampeyo confirms that Annie herself was an exceptional potter, worthy of the recognition that she has yet to receive.

Lesso's role in Nampeyo's pottery-making has become more

exaggerated and idealized with the passage of time. A mystique has been created comparing Nampeyo and Lesso with Maria Martinez and Julian of San Ildefonso Pueblo with no evidence of support. Born a full generation earlier than Julian and living in a relatively isolated culture, Lesso was a working farmer who butchered sheep and cattle, tanned hides, made moccasins, and performed other male chores at the ranch, on the mesa, and in the kiva. Ruth Bunzel, in her published studies of pueblo pottery during the summers of 1924 and 1925,[4] referred several times to Julian, who decorated Maria's vessels, and to their creation of a style of pottery of rare distinction. However, she credited Nampeyo alone for reviving an ancient pottery style with unerring discrimination and lively perception, and Lesso is mentioned nowhere in her text.

Lesso's death certificate states that he "polished and painted pottery for his wife,"[5] but no living family member with whom I talked is able to identify Lesso's painting, no visitor recorded having seen Lesso working on pottery, and he was never photographed with brush in hand to illustrate what designs he painted, how well he painted, or when he was painting for his wife. If he did, in fact, help to polish unfired pots or assist in painting them, the lack of any evidence of this confirms that Lesso was not as important to Nampeyo's work as the highly visible Annie.

A few vessels made by Nampeyo were signed, but they are the exception. The exterior of an early bowl, purchased by Frank and Clara Churchill around 1904–1907 (Hood Museum of Art, Dartmouth College, cat. #46-17-1011), is signed in unconnected script letters "Numpayo," but the catalog card for the item states that the signature appears to have been added after firing. Her other signed vessels, most of small size and later date, probably were identified with her printed name by one of her daughters for the Museum of Northern Arizona Hopi Craftsman exhibits in the early 1930s. None of the vessels were signed by Nampeyo herself because she was unable to write, nor did the early potters feel it necessary to identify their own work.

The painted decoration by each potter was in itself a signature as individual as handwriting. Many decades later, it is those "handwritings" of the past that are analyzed in order to attribute unsigned vessels. Common elements of design were available to all potters: triangles, squares, crescents, circles, scrolls, and so on. The way in which Nampeyo joined, overlaid, and interrelated the elements defines her personal style. Several descendants of Nampeyo have said that, in the old days, potters respected and did not appropriate each other's designs. It is, therefore, not only the recognizable designs but her artistic idiosyncrasies in uncommon designs that identify Nampeyo's hand.

Other elements also are significant in attribution. The various Hopi clays used by Nampeyo imparted their individual characteristics to the finished work. She used gray clay that fired to a cream-to-honey color and yellow clay that fired to a toasty orange-to-brick-red color. She varied the main body color occasionally with a white, yellow, or red slip over the gray clay. Because the Hopi clay cannot be molded with thin walls, her vessels sometimes feel heavy for their graceful appearance. This clay, however, does allow forms capable of severe flexures, which Nampeyo understood and, with her skill, used to advantage.

More abstract than design and form is the intuitive feeling one experiences after studying hundreds of vessels that Nampeyo's hands have shaped and decorated. Nampeyo was not an infallibly expert technician. She was a pioneer of an art form integrated from the styles of ancient potters who had passed centuries earlier. Her vessels were often heavy and many times not carefully smoothed inside. Frequently the striae on the bottom were left unpolished, and impurities not removed from her clay sometimes produced pits and spalls during firing. However, Nampeyo was invariably a master of effect. Each of her vessels has a marked sense of balance and grace in the visual connection between shape and design. When all the elements came together—the clay, the workmanship, the paint and design, the firing, and the concept—the vessels are unquestionably, exquisitely, and uniquely "Nampeyo."

Nampeyo made open "food" bowls throughout her life, for they were a traditional Hopi vessel, less expensive for collectors to purchase, and easier for visitors to carry than the more bulky jars. Early photos show her with deep U-shaped bowls with the sides gently sloping outward and an interior design (Figure 1). Other pre-1900 photos show bowls with spherical sides and a slightly everted rim with designs on both interior and exterior surfaces (Figure 2). The most typical shape after the turn of the century was fairly shallow (approximately 3 × 9 inches diameter) with an inward roll at the rim (Figure 3). They were in such demand that Herman Schweizer of the Fred Harvey Company would order two or three dozen at a time from Juan Lorenzo Hubbell.

Many interior decorations in bowls were variations of the exterior designs on her jars, but the flatter, less complex surface allowed her to improvise linear designs, symmetrical patterns, and abstract asymmetrical shapes not compatible with jar shapes. Within the bowl, a black band, the "framing line" or "road line," was frequently placed just below the rim.

Line-breaks in the framing line of bowls and jars can be found on very few vessels attributed to Nampeyo. A small jar with continuous panel design of stylized swastikas (atypical of Nampeyo's designs but suggestive of Annie's hand) dating to the early part of the century has a bold broken line both above and below the panel (Denver Art Museum, cat. #A29-436).

Painted rims also are extremely rare on Nampeyo's work. One member of the family said that Nampeyo never painted the rims of her vessels. A medium-size jar with eagle tail design and painted rim, however, was purchased at the turn of the century by Matthew Howell, a salesman in harness and saddlery (Arizona State Museum, cat. #E8996). Until a comparative study is made of more vessels attributed to Nampeyo with line-breaks and painted rims, it must be concluded that they are generally uncharacteristic of Nampeyo's painting.

Although an approximate chronology of Nampeyo's jars is possible, many atypical vessels are difficult to date or even to attribute: experimental shapes or designs not repeated; what may appear to be Nampeyo-shaped vessels otherwise lacking her idiosyncrasies of design; and other items, such as pitchers, ladles, rattles, and canteens. When she experimented or when she simply played with the clay, she produced pottery that may never be attributed to the best potter on First Mesa, for she was not a "manufacturer" of recognizable, salable clay vessels. She enjoyed her own talent and improvised continually, so that any analysis of her work must be conditional.

The chronological outline that follows is based on a study of several hundred vessels made by or attributed to Nampeyo in public collections, in private collections, and on the market. Many were well documented; others were attributed without provenance. Unfortunately, during her lifetime, Nampeyo's vessels were considered curios, not collectibles, so that few collectors recorded when the vessel was purchased or from whom. Many museum catalog cards note "Made by Nampeyo" without further explanation or documentation.

Dated photographs of Nampeyo with her pottery provide the most reliable identification of the type of vessels she was making at a given time, but most photographs date before World War I. Many photographs were undated, and it was necessary to judge her age to approximate the date they were taken.

It was essential also to evaluate the effect on Nampeyo's work of events in her private life and of historical changes on the Hopi Reservation and in the nation. Her life and work were directly affected by the dramatic transition on the mesas from isolation during her youth to tourist attraction before she died. And she did not produce throughout her later life the quantity, the quality, and the variety that she had produced in her younger years. Most important, her eye disease, presumably trachoma, first treated before 1900, gradually diminished her sight, so that by the mid-1920s she was no longer able to paint the jars and bowls that she shaped. The vessels made by her hands reflected phases in the life of their maker, a human being vulnerable to the effects of time and to cultural evolution.

With a chronology of her work established, attributing Nampeyo's undocumented work to a certain period is often possible. An artist does not paint a still life, then a landscape, and then a portrait; each requires a different feeling for the subject. Typically he undertakes a series of works of one genre and paints variations of a subject until his feeling for it has been fully expressed or has diminished. Nampeyo painted several favorite designs throughout her career, and the vessels on which they are painted can be difficult to date. However, she used other designs for short periods before abandoning them entirely. Together with shapes that she modified over time, painted designs frequently offer clues for dating her work. Vessels without provenance can be compared in shape and design with others of a known period, and if elements are similar, they may then be attributed to an approximate date.

The pottery that Nampeyo produced during her career falls into five distinct periods.

PERIOD 1 (PRE-1900)

Known examples of Nampeyo's pottery dating before 1900 are few, but they indicate that she was an expert potter who had not yet found her personal style. The earliest documentation are photographs taken in 1893 by James Mooney (Photographs 7 and 8), picturing Nampeyo with two bowls with spherical sides with continuous exterior fret designs. The simplified interior curvilinear designs with bold framing lines are similar in concept.

In 1896, Walter Hough made a collection of seven bowls, now in the collection of the National Museum of Natural History, Smithsonian Institution, Washington D.C. Three shapes are represented in the collection: one U-shaped bowl (Figure 1), one bowl with spherical sides and with everted rim (Figure 2), and bowls with inwardly rolled rim (Figure 3) (Plate 1). The latter shape was deeper than her typical later bowls, which emphasized the interior design, a shape that appealed to collectors. One was painted with a kachina face, two with kachina figures, and the remaining with linear or abstract designs.

Sumner Matteson's photograph of Nampeyo and Annie (Photograph 11) ca. 1900 or earlier provokes conjecture.[6] If the photograph proves to have been taken before 1900, it documents atypical vase-shaped jars and large open bowls made by Nampeyo during the late 1890s. Designs painted on them were more static and vessel shapes less graceful than her later ones.

At the time of Matteson's photograph, Annie would have been in her teens and still maturing as a potter. She is pictured holding a seed jar painted with two birds beak-to-beak at a trumpet-shaped flower. Another small jar with a similar design is on the floor in the foreground. This simple concept of double bird and flower motif was painted with variations on jars and canteens at later dates. I suggest that it was Annie's design and that vessels decorated with the motif were her vessels. As explained by family members, in the old days potters respected each other's designs and did not use them but created their own.

The most elegant example of Nampeyo's pre-1900 work is a large canteen (Arizona State Museum, Tucson, cat. #4099) (Plate 2) given to Dr. Joshua Miller in exchange for treating the potter's eyes. The canteen has a red slip back, neck, and handles, and a crackled white slip body painted with kachina face.

Period 1 appears to have been a transition for Nampeyo, as it was for all Hopi potters. Polacca Polychrome continued to be made, primarily for household use,[7] and the new revival style became the "commercial" product for sale to visitors. Until a more comparative study of pre-1900 vessels is made, data and examples that can be attributed to this period remain incomplete.

PERIOD 2 (CA. 1900–1910)

By 1900, Nampeyo was potting at her prime in a personal, contemporary style. During Period 2, the proficient, prolific potter improvised continually and produced more diversified work than in any later period.

Shapes

In 1900, Edward S. Curtis photographed Nampeyo with two large globose vessels (Figure 5) (Photograph 12). Two vessels of similar shape appear in A.C. Vroman's 1901 photograph of the potter (Photograph 13) surrounded by her work.

Though a few examples are extant (Denver Art Museum, cat. #1941.301, date unknown), this shape is not common in Nampeyo's major output. It is questionable, however, whether other potters might have accepted the challenge of making such an impressive coiled shape. Design elements on an unattributed vessel of this shape might substantiate it as Nampeyo's work.

Nampeyo's "signature" vessels were the large 18- to 20-inch diameter, low-profile, truncated-neck, Sikyatki-shape jars (Figure 6) first recorded in Vroman's photographs of 1901. Producing the flattened shoulders required great skill and patience in order to prevent the wet clay from collapsing as successive coils were added. This shape is most predominant in Periods 2 and 5.

Edward S. Curtis photographed Nampeyo around 1904 with three of the typical seed jars that she made throughout her life. All have a common shape: less than 7 inches in diameter and about 3 inches in height, the largest diameter at about the lower third of the jar. Side walls taper with slightly concave shoulders to a small orifice (Figure 7).

During this period, Nampeyo varied the shapes of her medium-size jars. Vroman's photographs of 1901 illustrate jars with spherical side walls (Figure 8). One shape predominant about 1903 was flatter in profile with more sharply angled upper and lower side walls. The widest diameter was about halfway between top and bottom, and the shoulder tapered to a short standing neck (Figure 9). Such jars were collected by artists Louis Akin and E. Irving Couse (Plate 5) in that year.

One medium-size jar of this period (American Museum of Natural History, cat. #29.0-257) is a precursor of Nampeyo's later medium-size jars with the widest diameter dropped to the lower third of the jar (Figure 10), similar in profile to but larger than her seed jars (Figure 7).

Except for her large-diameter, low-profile, Sikyatki-shaped jars, few large water jars of other shapes were documented during this period. One with a small base and angular lower and upper side walls (Figure 11) is painted with a graceful panel design (Mesa Verde Museum, cat. #MEVE3767) (Plate 21).

Designs

Whether a potter thinks "bird" or "feather" when she stylizes elements of a design to fit on a particular clay shape only she can say. For white men, if something exists, it must be named; a symbol must have a meaning. Was this also true of early Indian potters?[8] Nampeyo could not have explained in English her intentions as her yucca brush unhesitantly outlined a design on an unfired, polished vessel. In the following discussions, therefore, names commonly associated with particular designs are used for identification purposes only and do not imply an abstract symbolism expressed by Nampeyo.

The "eagle tail" design (Figure A) illustrates Nampeyo's improvisation, for she painted this design throughout her career, each time with variations. She painted the design with particular grace on her low-profile Sikyatki-shaped jars of Period 2, varying the red square around the orifice and the design in the rectangle above the extended "feathers." She varied the number of stylized feathers and occasionally introduced white into the black-and-red design. Two black scrolls swept apart from the corners of the red square that surrounded the orifice.

The rectangle above the extended feathers in the eagle tail design most frequently included "stars," which Nampeyo varied in number and shape. But for a short period, about 1904 to 1910, she incorporated a rectangle with diagonal and frets (Figure B) in many designs, occasionally substituting it for the star design in the eagle tail (Figure C). The diagonal-and-fret rectangle can be found within numerous designs on bowls and jars that were documented within a few short years during Period 1.

Nampeyo began integrating the "wingtip" element of the ancient migration design into innumerable improvised patterns (Figure D) during this period. She rarely painted the complete design (Figure E) in the repetitive manner of her descendants, but rather added stylized extending feathers and scrolls, incorporated a clown face, and stippled or decorated the interlocking bands. She exhibited an impatience to embellish the rigid pattern.

The stylized bird or "spider" design (Figure F) appears on a seed jar in the foreground of a photo taken by Edward S. Curtis as early as 1904, and it reappears with modifications in bowl interiors, on medium-size water jars, and on at least one globose storage jar (Museum of Indian Arts and Culture, Santa Fe, cat. #7721.12) (Plate 8). This design may have been confined to Period 2.

Nampeyo was adept at placing five designs equidistant around a jar. One water jar of this period is painted with a panel design of two graceful motifs repeated five times between two heavy black framing lines (Mesa Verde Museum, cat. #MEVE3767) (Plate 21). Panel decoration, however, was rarely painted by Nampeyo's hand, for she excelled at creating negative space (the space left unpainted) in her designs. Panel designs appear to have been too confining, too restrictive for her individualistic expression.

Strangely, Nampeyo's work from the latter half of this period is largely undocumented. She traveled twice to Hopi House at the Grand Canyon (1905 and 1907) and once to Chicago (1910) to demonstrate her pottery-making, but except for two photos taken at Hopi House in 1905, I have found no photos of the potter and her work or vessels dated specifically to these few latter years.

PERIOD 3 (CA. 1910–1917)

By 1910, Nampeyo's reputation was established and her pottery was in demand. She was producing for a market of collectors.

Annie had matured into a fine potter, and during this period the first documented pots made by Annie were collected by artist William R. Leigh (Gilcrease Museum). Samuel Barrett wrote in 1911 that the best pottery at First Mesa was produced by Nampeyo and Annie ("Kwe tca we"), who were assisted by Lesso and other younger members of the family. Lesso may have polished unfired, unpainted vessels for them both, but as explained earlier in the text, he was never seen or photographed actually painting a vessel. The younger members to whom Barrett referred may have been Nampeyo's fifteen-year-old Nellie and eleven-year-old Fannie, and Annie's ten-year-old Rachel.

Period 3 ended abruptly when visitors disappeared from the mesas during World War I.

Shapes

The shapes of Nampeyo's medium-size jars changed from those made during Period 2. The base of the vessels was generally larger and more flatly rounded. Lower side walls did not angle outward from the base as sharply as in Period 2. Because of the flat-rounded bottoms, the widest diameter of many of her jars of this period is at the lower third of the jar. Shoulders are slightly concave, tapering to the orifice (Figure 10).

A few jars of this period have a deeply rounded base terminating in almost flat shoulders and truncated neck (Figure 12), a shape that does not appear in other periods. Two examples (School of American Research, cat. #297, and Gilcrease Museum, cat. #5437.4423) are painted with similar designs that have faded in the same manner.

Nampeyo abandoned the low-profile Sikyatki-style jars during this period, but her large jars were impressive in size nevertheless. She pulled the walls up for greater height, the largest diameter being about halfway between the orifice and the more deeply rounded bottom (Figure 13). This practice reduced the risk of wet clay walls collapsing as coils were added and tended to make large vessels seem plump rather than sleek.

Designs

The first documented "bat-wing" design (Figure G) that I found is in the Samuel Barrett 1911 collection at the Milwaukee Public Museum. During Period 3, Nampeyo painted this design on both small seed jars and large jars (Plate 11), particularly those shaped as in Figure 13. Several large red-slipped jars painted with black or black-and-white bat-wing designs are extant, which indicates the work of Annie, who, as previously noted, frequently painted black or black-and-white designs on red slip.

The design of a circular motif (Figure H) seems to have been confined to the years 1912 to 1915. It appears both free-floating, one on either side of the jar (School of American Research, cat. #3011) (Plate 22), and in conjunction with an A-shaped stylized kachina design (Figure I).

Nampeyo and Annie were sharing motifs by Period 3, for Annie also used the stylized kachina design. The comparison of two jars collected by William R. Leigh in 1912 illustrates the difference in style between Nampeyo's handwork (Gilcrease Museum, cat. #5437.4396) (Plate 9) and Annie's work (Gilcrease Museum, cat. #5437.4420) (Plate 10). Nampeyo's jar is painted with two black-and-red kachina designs alternated with two circle motifs on a white slip. Annie's is painted with four black kachina designs on a red slip. Nampeyo's is bold; Annie's is almost minimal and more delicate. Both vessels are masterful examples of each potter's talent, and each expresses the personality of its maker.

PERIOD 4 (CA. 1917–1930)

World War I galvanized the nation, but life for the residents on the isolated mesas quietly continued without outsiders photographing, observing ceremonies, or purchasing handcrafts. When tourists returned, they wanted inexpensive souvenirs. At this time, Nampeyo's trachoma, which alternately went into remission and then recurred, gradually diminished her eyesight.

Shapes

While visitors were absent from the mesa and probably to compensate for her failing vision, Nampeyo experimented with more tactile designs and shapes. A photograph taken around 1920 by Emry Kopta shows Nampeyo with a jar with a corrugated neck (Photograph 24), the first evidence of corrugation in her work. Other jars with corrugations that I have seen date to this period, around 1918 to 1922 (Plate 13). Her sense of whimsy expressed itself in corrugated bulges pushed out in the side walls or shoulders of other jars, perhaps to indicate ears of corn (Plate 15). One such jar, which suffers badly from deterioration, is located in the front left bedroom of Hubbell's ranch house at the Hubbell Trading Post in Ganado.

Several sensational large storage jars (Figure 14) without provenance indicate Nampeyo's hand (Arizona State Museum, cat. #52543 with square orifice, for example) (Plate 14). The lack of documentation for such jars and of photographs picturing them leaves their date of origin in question. Until more evidence becomes available, I suggest that these masterfully crafted jars were made during early Period 4. Without buyers for her work during the war, Nampeyo probably took the vessels to trader Tom Pavatea, who, with little possibility of selling them himself, traded the vessels to other posts where they were purchased years later, provenance unknown.

When tourists returned to the mesas after the war, they wanted only inexpensive souvenirs, and potters complied, producing ashtrays, ceramic cowboy hats and boots, amorphous pots, and other nontraditional items. Nampeyo, too, succumbed to the market and, for a short period of time, made effigies (Phoebe Hearst Museum of Anthropology, cat. #2-47043) and rain gods (Plate 23). The rain gods were similar to those made in Tesuque Pueblo, New Mexico, but where Nampeyo had seen them is unknown.

By 1925 or 1926, Ruth Bunzel reported that Nampeyo "makes no modern white forms, no worthless trifles. She makes only dignified pieces in the best traditional style."[9] One informant who visited the potter in 1928 saw several small pots that were to be taken by a Fred Harvey Company representative to Hopi House at the Grand Canyon for sale. Without current evidence, however, the shapes of the traditional vessels that Nampeyo made during the 1920s is not known.

Designs

Aware of diminishing eyesight, when does an artist stop painting? Gradually, with the hope that sight will again improve. Indications are that Nampeyo continued to paint to the best of her ability for several years into the 1920s, which would account for some extant vessels with seemingly careless brushwork.

In the mid-1920s, Ruth Bunzel wrote that Nampeyo's "designs are executed with greater delicacy and precision and her line work is superior to that of her fellow workers. Furthermore, her designs are of a different character. There is less design per square inch of pot. At times her patterns are almost impressionistic in their economy."[10] Bunzel described other designs as "very much cruder."[11]

Bunzel appears to have seen the painting of more than one hand; her descriptions are contradictory. Nampeyo's own and by then infrequent painting could have been considered cruder. Annie's painting would have evinced greater delicacy and superior line work. The different character may have been the handwork of Lena Charlie, who lived on the plaza in Hano. A family member explained that her father was Corn clan, so she was a niece of Nampeyo. Lena herself was a potter, but she did not paint in the Nampeyo style. Her designs were less complex, frequently with large shapes in the overall pattern painted red. Many of her design elements emanated from the bottom framing line. One of Nampeyo's descendants identified a globose vessel made by Nampeyo but painted with uncharacteristic design (Museum of Indian Arts and Culture, Santa Fe, cat. #11020/12) as having been painted by Lena.

A number of extant vessels attributed to Nampeyo are painted with static panel designs between two framing lines. The panels contain geometric shapes against painted or stippled negative areas, so that the panel appears completely filled in. The concept lacks Nampeyo's sense of space and spontaneity and was, without doubt, the painting of another person. The vessels themselves may have been shaped by Nampeyo during the 1920s, but more study will have to determine who painted them.

During Period 4, Nampeyo's jars were no longer the signature vessels of earlier periods. She experimented with more tactile shapes during the war years. When visitors returned to the mesa, she was not seeing well enough to paint competently, and other members of the family began painting her vessels for her.

PERIOD 5 (CA. 1930–1942)

Lesso died in 1930, a "feeble man. Had crippled arm."[12] During this period of her life, the aging Nampeyo must have been severely restricted in her pottery-making. Besides caring for an infirm husband, she could not have dug clay and carried it home, nor could she see well enough to paint the few pots that she could make. By the mid-1930s, Nampeyo seems to have begun potting with renewed interest, supplied with clay by members of the family. She was still shaping vessels in 1939, three years before her death.

Shapes

Nampeyo apparently continued to make pottery even during difficult personal times. From 1930 to 1934, she entered small vessels signed with her name on the bottom (presumably by whichever daughter had painted the pot) in the Museum of Northern Arizona Hopi Craftsman exhibits. By the mid-1930s, Nampeyo again began making the large-diameter, low-profile, Sikyatki-shape jars that had earned her reputation at the turn of the century (Plate 16).

Designs

Though Nampeyo never lost total vision, she was unable to paint her vessels by this period and relied on others to do so: Annie, who painted and fired her mother's vessels at the ranch; Fannie, who had moved to Keams Canyon with her husband, Vinton; granddaughter Daisy, who had left the reservation as a young teenager to have eye surgery, had become a protégée of Anita Baldwin, and had returned to First Mesa about 1930; and Lena Charlie, a niece who lived in Hano. Perhaps others assisted Nampeyo as well. It may not have mattered to the old lady. "She didn't know she was important at the time."[13]

SUMMARY

Departing from the Polacca Polychrome style of ceramics made on the Hopi mesas during her youth, Nampeyo was working in a revival style by 1893,[14] stimulated, as many potters were, by the aggressive collecting of artifacts by the National Museum during the 1880s. By 1900, Nampeyo had created a personal, contemporary style known only as "Hopi Revival" pottery during her lifetime. She was prolific; she had an artist's eye of balance. She had a sense of whimsy; she continually improvised.

Nampeyo's work can be divided into five distinct periods:

Period 1 (Pre-1900). Few photographs and vessels from this period are extant, but it can be deduced that Nampeyo had not yet found a personal style.

Period 2 (ca. 1900–1910). Nampeyo was potting at her prime, continually improvising more varied work than in any other period.

Period 3 (ca. 1910–1917). Nampeyo was producing for a market of collectors. Vessels show fine workmanship but less improvisation.

Period 4 (ca. 1917–1930). With diminishing eyesight, Nampeyo produced more tactile work in corrugations and shapes. This is the least documented period of the potter's life.

Period 5 (ca. 1930–1942). Nampeyo continued to shape vessels that others painted for her. She returned to making the large-diameter, flat-shouldered jars she had made at the turn of the century.

Belatedly in 1956, the revival style of pottery that Nampeyo had perfected was designated "Hano Polychrome,"[15] in recognition of the village in which it had originated and in tribute to the potter who had refined it into a contemporary style.

This study of Nampeyo's pottery is only a beginning. Further work in the following fields will augment the information contained in this text:

1. Relating the elements of Nampeyo's designs to the prehistoric styles from which they were borrowed.

2. More analysis to identify Annie's vessels and to correct erroneous attributions to Nampeyo in early collections.

3. Locating as yet unknown dated photographs of the potter that may show additional examples of her work.

4. Applying all of the known data, a more accurate attribution of vessels to the potter and to the periods in which she made them must be made.

The old lady would have been amused by all of these words describing and catagorizing her work. She did not comprehend her importance in revitalizing Hopi pottery. For her, there was only a timeless compulsion to keep her hands busy with the clay in a revival style now known as Hano Polychrome.

Profiles of Vessels

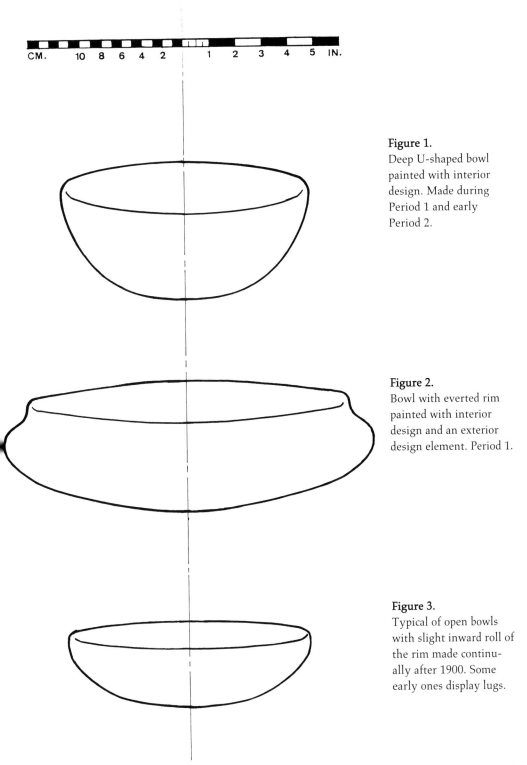

CM. 10 8 6 4 2 1 2 3 4 5 IN.

Figure 1.
Deep U-shaped bowl
painted with interior
design. Made during
Period 1 and early
Period 2.

Figure 2.
Bowl with everted rim
painted with interior
design and an exterior
design element. Period 1.

Figure 3.
Typical of open bowls
with slight inward roll of
the rim made continu-
ally after 1900. Some
early ones display lugs.

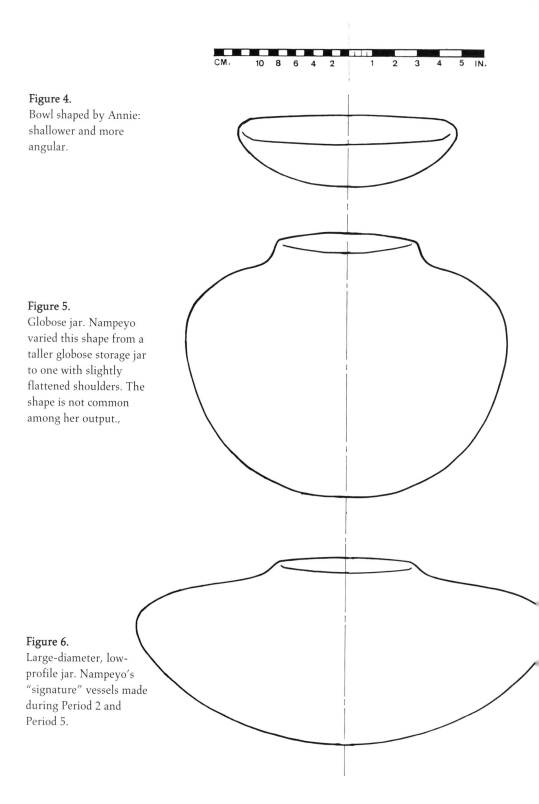

CM. 10 8 6 4 2 1 2 3 4 5 **IN.**

Figure 4.
Bowl shaped by Annie:
shallower and more
angular.

Figure 5.
Globose jar. Nampeyo
varied this shape from a
taller globose storage jar
to one with slightly
flattened shoulders. The
shape is not common
among her output.,

Figure 6.
Large-diameter, low-
profile jar. Nampeyo's
"signature" vessels made
during Period 2 and
Period 5.

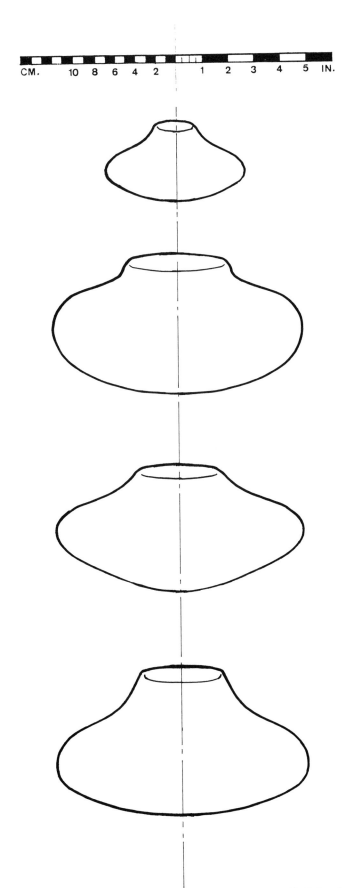

CM. 10 8 6 4 2   1 2 3 4 5 IN.

Figure 7.
Typical seed jar with largest diameter at about the lower third of the jar, side walls tapering with slightly concave shoulders to a small orifice.

Figure 8.
Medium-size jar with spherical side walls, made during Period 2.

Figure 9.
Medium-size jar with more sharply angled upper and lower side walls, the widest diameter being halfway between top and bottom. Made during early Period 2.

Figure 10.
Medium-size jar with widest diameter dropped to the lower third of the jar. Made primarily during Period 3.

Stylistic Analysis of Vessels / 181

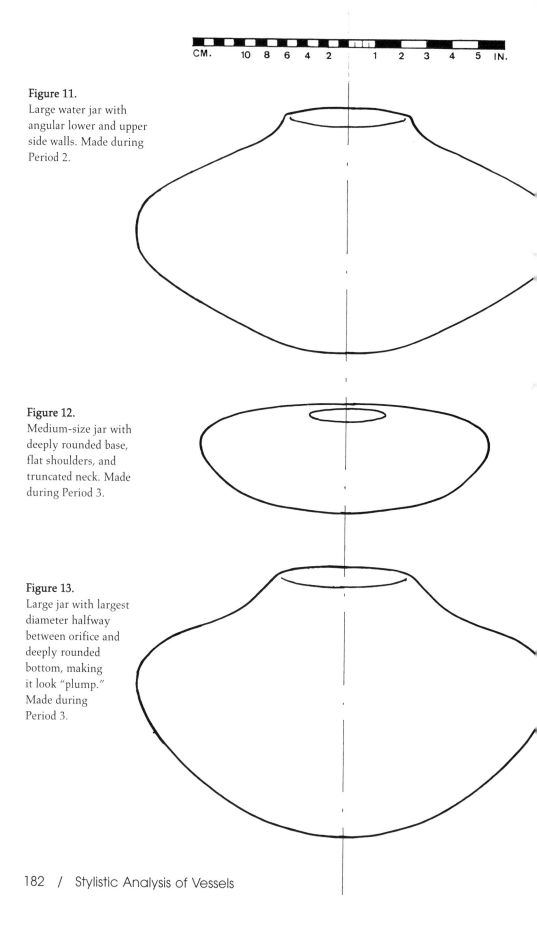

Figure 11.
Large water jar with angular lower and upper side walls. Made during Period 2.

Figure 12.
Medium-size jar with deeply rounded base, flat shoulders, and truncated neck. Made during Period 3.

Figure 13.
Large jar with largest diameter halfway between orifice and deeply rounded bottom, making it look "plump." Made during Period 3.

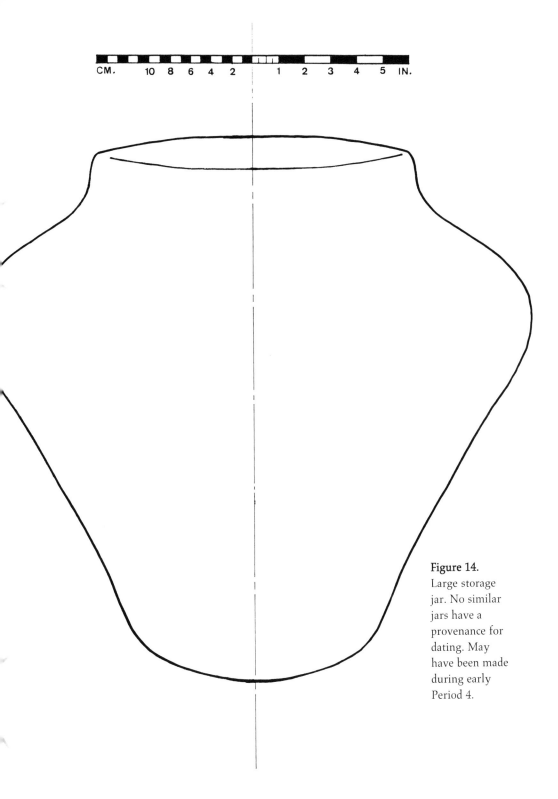

CM. 10 8 6 4 2   1 2 3 4 5 IN.

Figure 14.
Large storage
jar. No similar
jars have a
provenance for
dating. May
have been made
during early
Period 4.

Common Designs

Figure A.
Eagle Tail design.
Nampeyo painted this
design throughout her
career, improvising
continually.

Figure B.
Rectangle with diagonal
and frets. Nampeyo
incorporated a rectangle
with diagonal and frets
into various designs for
bowls and on jars,
improvising the ele-
ments, for a short period
around 1904 to 1910,
Period 2.

Figure C.
Eagle Tail with rectangle with diagonal and frets. Replacing the usual rectangle with stars with a rectangle with diagonal and frets in the Eagle Tail, Nampeyo painted several red slip jars with this design around 1904 to 1910, Period 2.

Figure D.
Wingtip element. Nampeyo incorporated the wingtip and feather element in many designs, with clown faces (as shown), with scrolls, and with stippled or decorated interlocking bands.

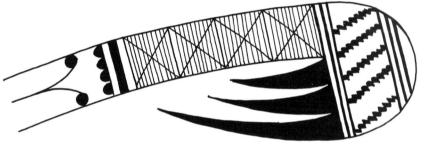

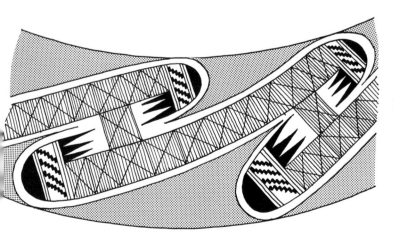

Figure E.
Migration design. Nampeyo rarely painted the complete migration design on her jars, showing an impatience to embellish the rigid pattern.

Figure F.
Spider design. This design is seen on a seed jar in a Curtis photograph as early as 1904, and it reappears with modifications in bowls and jars during Nampeyo's early work.

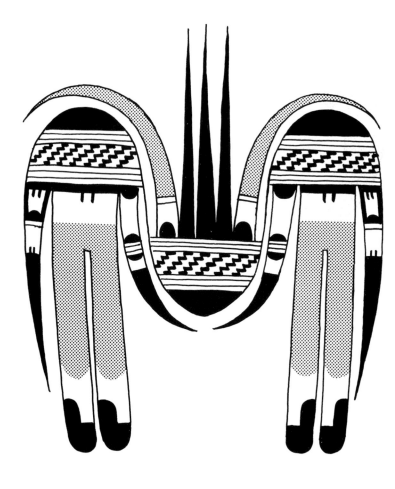

Figure G.
Batwing design. Nampeyo painted this design on seed jars, medium-size jars, and the large "plump" jars of Period 3.

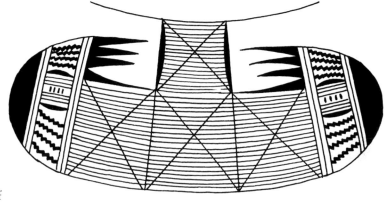

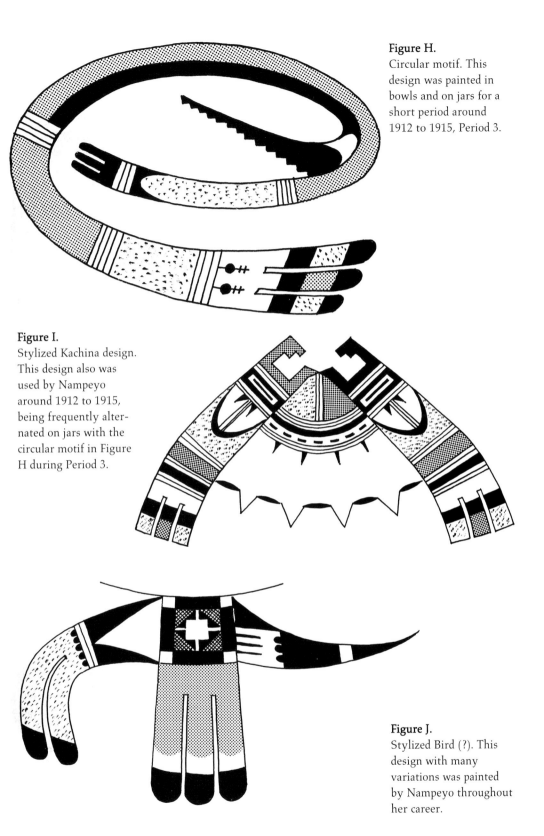

Figure H.
Circular motif. This design was painted in bowls and on jars for a short period around 1912 to 1915, Period 3.

Figure I.
Stylized Kachina design. This design also was used by Nampeyo around 1912 to 1915, being frequently alternated on jars with the circular motif in Figure H during Period 3.

Figure J.
Stylized Bird (?). This design with many variations was painted by Nampeyo throughout her career.

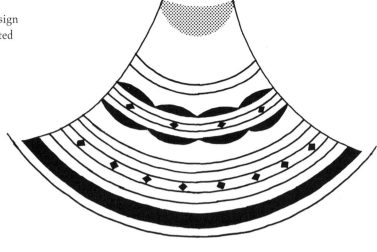

Figure K.
Stylized Kilt (?). This design with variations was painted by Nampeyo primarily during Period 3.

Figure L.
Clown face. Nampeyo whimsically tucked variations of the clown face into many designs throughout her career.

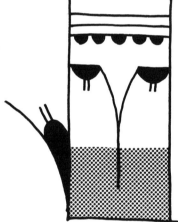

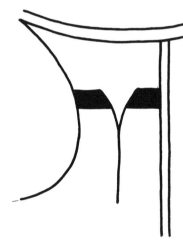

Appendix A:
Published Fallacies
and Erroneous Photographs

By definition, history is a record of significant past events and an explanation of their causes. When published reports concern a potter and a people who are isolated by both geography and language, the historical commentary is vulnerable to error and subjective interpretation.

As a traditional Hopi-Tewa unable to read the English language, Nampeyo could not deny inaccuracies about her and her pottery written by outsiders. The errors compounded by subsequent interpretations and embellishments have created a myth about the potter that has been uncritically repeated for over half a century. These are some of the major fallacies:

1. *That Nampeyo's Hopi grandmother in Walpi taught her how to make pottery* (Nequatewa, "Nampeyo, Famous Hopi Potter," 88).

Hopi and Hopi-Tewa mothers and daughters share a close bond, not only of familial relationship but also of clan. Maternal grandmothers and mothers pass on clan traditions and teach domestic chores to the daughters of the family. Nampeyo did not speak Hopi when she was young, which precludes a close relationship with her paternal Hopi Snake clan grandmother in Walpi. She learned how to pot from her Corn clan mother. (See Chapter 2.)

2. *That Nampeyo was married to another man before Lesso* (Nequatewa, "Nampeyo, Famous Hopi Potter," 88).

The story of a first marriage bears a remarkable resemblance to many oral legends in which a youth martyrs himself because of unrequited love of a maiden. (See Notes, Chapter 3, no. 4.)

3. *That Nampeyo's husband, Lesso, worked for the archaeologist Jesse Walter Fewkes at the Sikyatki excavation in 1895* (Hough, "A Revival of the Ancient Hopi Pottery Art," 322).

All of Fewkes's reports about the excavation mention Lesso only as the husband who accompanied Nampeyo to the site to copy designs from the ancient ware. Twenty-two years after the excavation, in 1917, Walter Hough, who was not present at Sikyatki, added the embellishment of Lesso's employment by Fewkes. (See Chapter 13.)

4. *That the revival of Hopi pottery originated in 1895 when Jesse Walter Fewkes excavated Sikyatki* (Fewkes, "Preliminary Account," 557).

In the *Hopi Journal of Alexander M. Stephen*, Stephen recorded in January of 1893, that Nampeyo was making designs after those she had seen on ancient ware (130). (See Chapter 3 for stimulus of the revival.)

5. *That Thomas Keam played a major role in the revival of ancient pottery styles* (Wade, *America's Great Lost Expedition*, 75).

The twenty reproductions of prehistoric jars that Keam commissioned for unknown reasons were an insignificant number compared with the thousands of ancient vessels carried away by the National Museum in 1879 and the 1880s, which affected every household in seven villages on all three mesas. (See Chapter 3 for the stimulus of the revival.)

6. *That Lesso was as important to Nampeyo's pottery-making as Julian was to Maria Martinez of San Ildefonso Pueblo* (Nequatewa, "Nampeyo, Famous Hopi Potter," 90; Robert Ashton,

Jr., 1976, "Nampeyo and Lesou," *American Indian Art* 1(3):24–33).

Lesso was a working farmer who never was photographed or witnessed shaping or painting clay vessels. (See Chapter 17 for family participation in Nampeyo's pottery-making.)

7. *That Nampeyo attended a Santa Fe Railway Exhibition in Chicago in 1898* (Nequatewa, "Nampeyo, Famous Hopi Potter," 90).

No such exhibition existed. (See Notes, Chapter 7, no. 13.)

8. *That Mennonite missionary H.R. Voth assisted in building Nampeyo's reputation* (Walker and Wyckoff, *Hopis, Tewas, and the American Road*, 91).

There is no evidence in Voth's diary or papers of any relationship to or interest in Nampeyo. (See Chapter 7.)

9. *That Nampeyo's brother Tom Polacca operated a store around which the village of Polacca grew* (Ortiz, *Handbook of North American Indians. Southwest. Vol. 9*, 588).

Tom Polacca had alienated First Mesa residents, who would not have patronized a trading post operated by him. (See Chapter 7.)

10. *That Lesso died in 1932* (Nequatewa, "Nampeyo, Famous Hopi Potter," 42).

Lesso's death certificate shows death on May 7, 1930.

Errors have also been made in identifying other Hopi women in photographs as Nampeyo. The study of facial features, personal adornments, and vessels (if they are included in the photograph) would make identification more accurate.

Two photographs ca. 1910 in the collection of the Museum of New Mexico Photo Archives (see Linda B. Eaton, 1993, *Native American Art of the Southwest*, Publications International, Ltd., 81 and 82), for example, are of another potter identified as Nampeyo. The youthful facial features are not those of the fifty-year-old Nampeyo, the jar the woman is holding does not bear any of Nampeyo's elements, Nampeyo as a young potter was never photographed "in costume" as this potter was, and no wall hangings appear in any photographs of the interior of Nampeyo's home. Other photos that have come to my attention as being rare or unpublished have not been of Nampeyo.

Who were these other potters? They are deserving of their own identification. Where are the vessels that they made? Do they remain unattributed or have some of them mistakenly been attributed to Nampeyo?

It is unfortunate that no comparative study of potters and their pottery was made at the time. The weakness of our culture of focusing on known names and personalities has impeded the later critical analysis of other potters who may have been just as talented but overlooked.

Appendix B:
Genealogy

For more complete genealogy of descendants, see Rick Dillingham, *Fourteen Families in Pueblo Pottery,* 14–15. (Albuquerque, University of New Mexico Press, 1994)

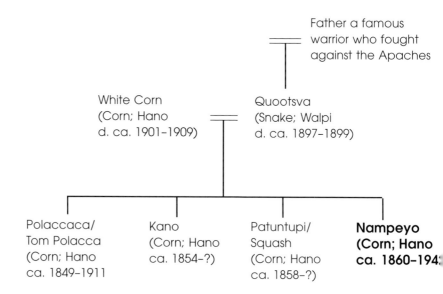

Father a famous warrior who fought against the Apaches

White Corn
(Corn; Hano
d. ca. 1901–1909)

Quootsva
(Snake; Walpi
d. ca. 1897–1899)

Polaccaca/
Tom Polacca
(Corn; Hano
ca. 1849–1911

Kano
(Corn; Hano
ca. 1854–?)

Patuntupi/
Squash
(Corn; Hano
ca. 1858–?)

**Nampeyo
(Corn; Hano
ca. 1860–194:**

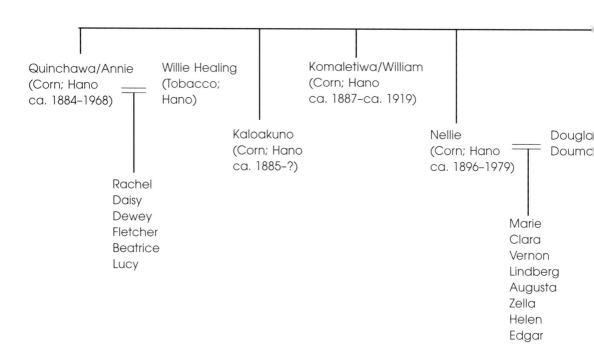

Quinchawa/Annie
(Corn; Hano
ca. 1884–1968)

Willie Healing
(Tobacco;
Hano)

Komaletiwa/William
(Corn; Hano
ca. 1887–ca. 1919)

Kaloakuno
(Corn; Hano
ca. 1885–?)

Nellie
(Corn; Hano
ca. 1896–1979)

Dougla
Douma

Rachel
Daisy
Dewey
Fletcher
Beatrice
Lucy

Marie
Clara
Vernon
Lindberg
Augusta
Zella
Helen
Edgar

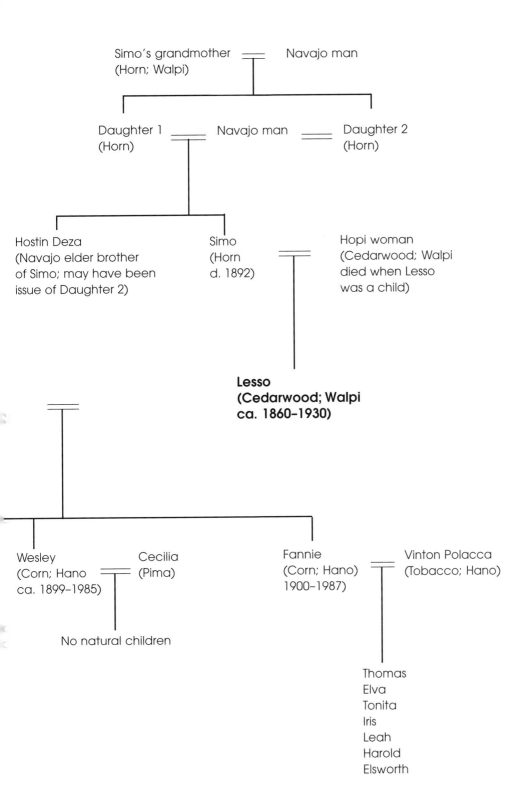

Simo's grandmother ═══ Navajo man
(Horn; Walpi)

Daughter 1 ───── Navajo man ───── Daughter 2
(Horn)   (Horn)

Hostin Deza   Simo   Hopi woman
(Navajo elder brother   (Horn   (Cedarwood; Walpi
of Simo; may have been   d. 1892)   died when Lesso
issue of Daughter 2)   was a child)

Lesso
(Cedarwood; Walpi
ca. 1860–1930)

Wesley   Cecilia   Fannie   Vinton Polacca
(Corn; Hano ═══ (Pima)   (Corn; Hano) ═══   (Tobacco; Hano)
ca. 1899–1985)   1900–1987)

No natural children   Thomas
                                             Elva
                                             Tonita
                                             Iris
                                             Leah
                                             Harold
                                             Elsworth

Appendix C:
Maps

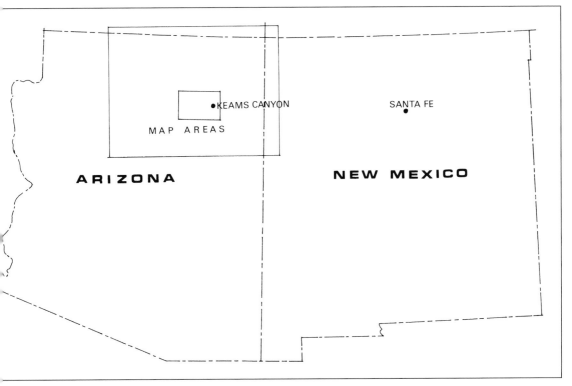

KEAMS CANYON

SANTA FE

MAP AREAS

ARIZONA

NEW MEXICO

Key Map

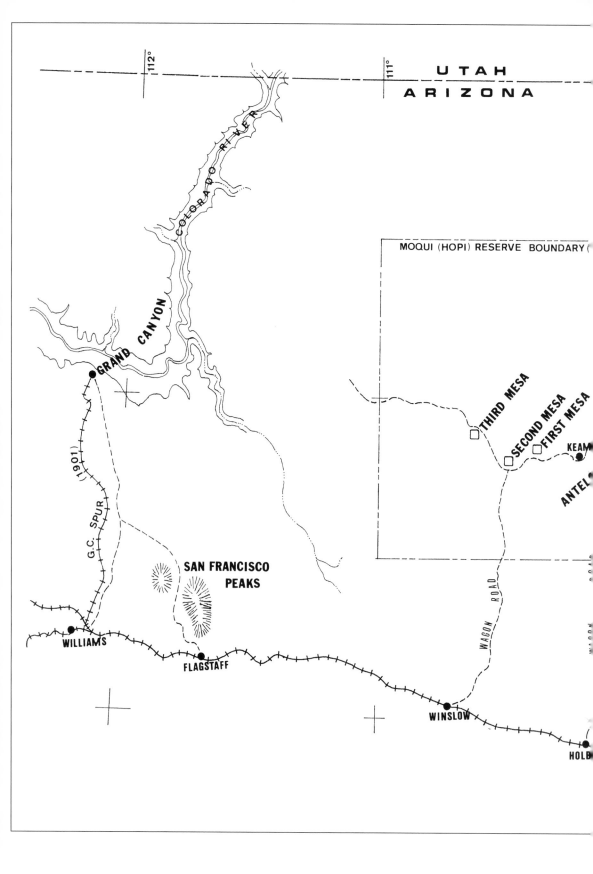

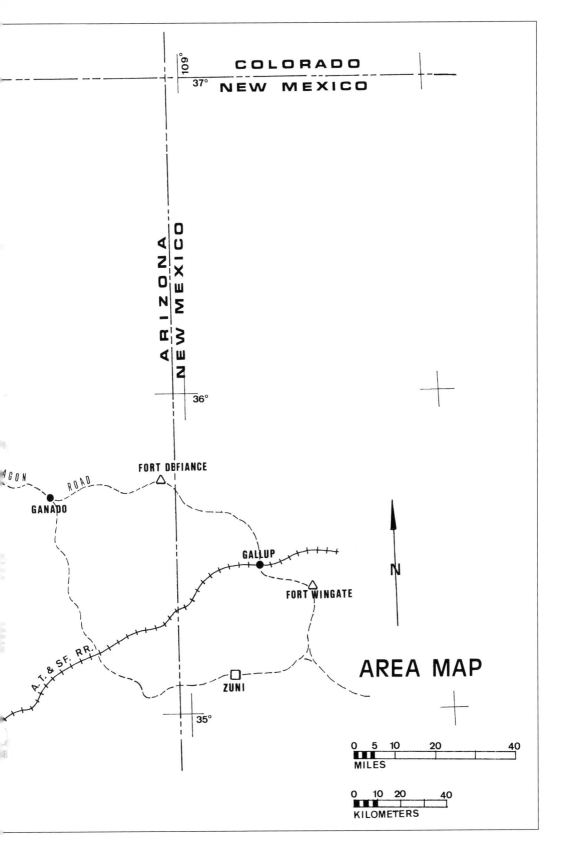

COLORADO

NEW MEXICO

109°

37°

ARIZONA

NEW MEXICO

36°

FORT DEFIANCE

AGON   ROAD

GANADO

GALLUP

FORT WINGATE

N

A. T. & S. F. RR.

ZUNI

35°

AREA MAP

0   5   10   20   40
◼◼◼◼
MILES

0   10   20   40
◼◼◼
KILOMETERS

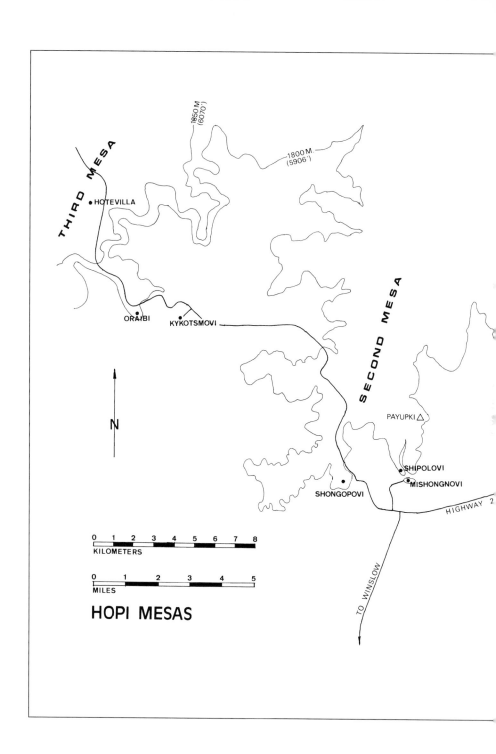

THIRD MESA

1850 M.
(6070')

1800 M.
(5906')

• HOTEVILLA

SECOND MESA

• ORAIBI
• KYKOTSMOVI

PAYUPKI △

N

• SHIPOLOVI
• MISHONGNOVI

• SHONGOPOVI

HIGHWAY 2

0 1 2 3 4 5 6 7 8
KILOMETERS

0   1   2   3   4   5
MILES

TO WINSLOW

HOPI MESAS

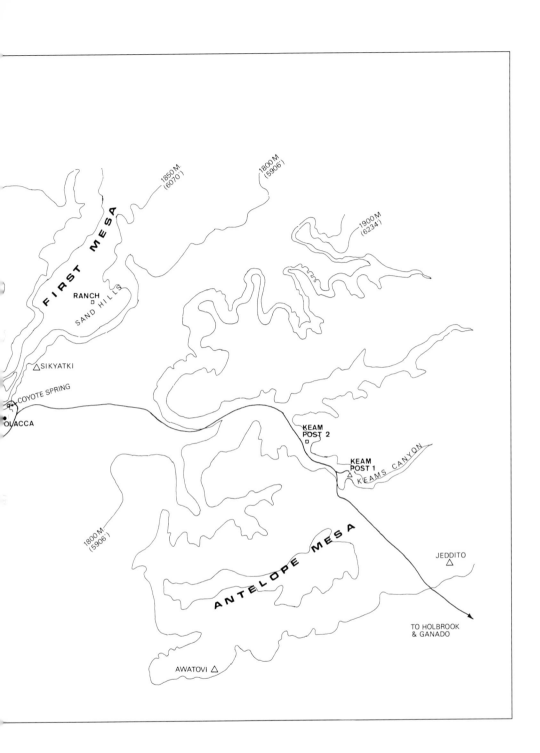

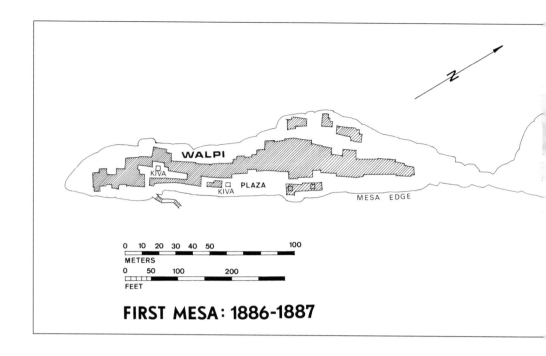

FIRST MESA: 1886-1887

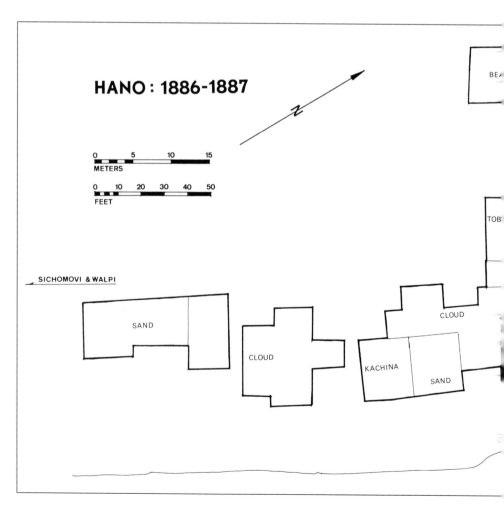

HANO: 1886-1887

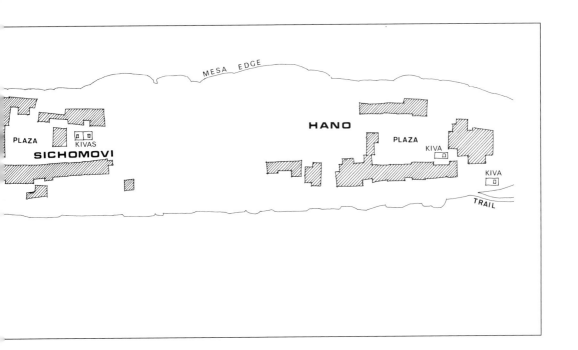

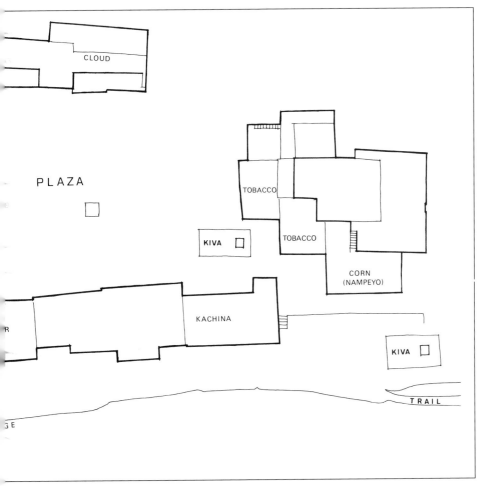

Notes

(Full reference for note sources will be found in the bibliography.)

Author's Notes and Acknowledgments

1. Nampeyo's second grandchild, Daisy, born about 1905 to Nampeyo's eldest daughter, Annie, suffered from a painful eye ailment when she was a girl. Anita Baldwin, whose father, Lucky Baldwin, had inherited a fortune, took Daisy to Los Angeles for eye surgery. Daisy stayed with Baldwin through her high-school years and then was enrolled in L'Ecole des Beaux Arts in Paris. At the conclusion of her studies, Daisy was taken around the world by Anita so she could experience the great art of many countries. When Daisy returned home to First Mesa, she decided to remain with her family and to learn how to pot in the traditional Hopi style. Daisy lived the last decades of her life in Zuni with her husband, Sydney Hooee. She died on November 29, 1994.

2. Dewey Healing was Nampeyo's first grandson, born to Annie about 1906 after Rachel and Daisy. Like his granduncle, Nampeyo's brother Tom Polacca, Dewey became an outspoken leader of the Hopi-Tewa people. In 1961, he was chairman of the Hopi Tribal Council when the tribe sued the Navajo Nation (*Healing vs. Jones*) in an attempt to remove Navajos from certain Hopi lands, a dispute that has not been settled at this writing. Dewey was son-in-law of Albert Yava, author of *Big Falling Snow*, and the husband of Juanita, whose mother, Ida, accompanied Nampeyo, Lesso, and Nellie to Chicago in 1910. Dewey died on April 11, 1992.

Chapter 1. Birth

1. For the legend of their emergence and other Hopi narratives told in their own words, see Courlander, *Hopi Voices*.

2. For the legend of the migration of the Tewas from their pueblo in New Mexico to Hopi, see Courlander, *The Fourth World of the Hopis*, 164–74.

3. Hough, *The Hopi Indians*, 76.

4. George C. Yount, "A Sketch of the Hopi in 1828."

5. Dr. P. S. G. Ten Broeck, U.S. Bureau of the Census, *Eleventh Census, Extra Census Bulletin*, 25–27.

6. James A. Little, *Jacob Hamblin: A Narrative of His Personal Experience as a Frontiersman, Missionary to the Indians and Explorer*.

7. Spelling varies from Quootsva to Kuichve.

8. Spelling of her Tewa name varies from Kolootsee to Kotcaka.

9. A greeting that means "How are you? I'm glad to see you. You're looking good."

10. Before 1900, the Hano Tewa ceremonial cycle was independent of Hopi influence. After the Tewa Sun clan became extinct and the office of Sun Watcher disappeared, Hano clans necessarily relied on the Walpi chief to announce the time for ceremonies to begin. Since that time, Hano ceremonies have been losing their own identity and becoming more akin to those of the Hopi.

11. Stephen, *Hopi Journal*, 534.

12. Natalie Curtis, *The Indians Book*, 473.

Chapter 2. Youth

1. Stephen, *Hopi Journal*, 1020.
2. Dewey Healing, quoted in Courlander, *Hopi Voices*, 121–22.
3. Burbank and Royce, *Burbank among the Indians*, 74.
4. Referring to family and clan members as well as to neighbors, Edmund Nequatewa used the term "jealousy" frequently in his memoirs, *Born A Chief*. An editor's footnote (number 27, page 57) states: "Gossip as a form of social control is probably universal. In Hopi society it is a finely honed art."
5. Freire-Marreco, "Tewa Kinship Terms from the Pueblo of Hano, Arizona," 283.
6. Ibid., 284.
7. Hodge, Notebook of Sikyatki Excavation. Wednesday, July 24, 1895.
8. U.S. Department of the Interior, *Annual Report of the Commissioner of Indian Affairs to the Secretary of the Interior, 1880–81*, 4.
9. Ibid., 1873. 286.
10. For more detailed information about Thomas Keam's activities as a trader, see Laura L. Graves's dissertation *Thomas Varker Keam*.
11. Jackson, *The Pioneer Photographer*, 256.
12. Ibid., 256–59.
13. U.S. Bureau of the Census, *Eleventh Census, Extra Census Bulletin*, 25–27.
14. Mindeleff, "A Study of Pueblo Architecture," 92–93.

Chapter 3. Marriage

1. Although the name has been spelled "Lesou" in recent years, the family pronounces the name "Less-oh," his children were given the surname "Lesso" in school, and the name on his death certificate is spelled "Lesso."
2. See Appendix B, Genealogy.
3. Mateer to the Commissioner of Indian Affairs, July 1, 1878. National Archives Microfilm Publication M234, roll 21. Bureau of Indian Affairs, Record Group 75, National Archives, Washington, D.C.

   Whereas European and American custom considered the husband the head of the family for genealogies or censuses, Hopis and Hopi-Tewas considered the oldest woman, the saja, the head of the family because clan was passed from mother to her children.
4. Ibid. In the article, "Nampeyo, Famous Hopi Potter," published after her death, Edmund Nequatewa wrote that about 1879 Nampeyo married a man by the name of Kwi-vio-ya, who left her because she was too pretty, and that she married Lesso two years later. The census taken in 1878 by Indian agent Mateer does not list a Kwi-vio-ya, or a name of any similar phonetic spelling, residing in any of the three villages on First Mesa. It does list Lesso, who had been born in Walpi, already living in "Tagua or 1st Village."
5. In 1891, Alexander Stephen listed Lesso as living in "Tewa." *Hopi Journal of Alexander M. Stephen*, 993.
6. Bunzel, *The Pueblo Potter*, 56.
7. In 1838, Englishman James Smithson bequeathed funds for the establishment of an institution bearing his name in the United States, a country he had never visited. Congress accepted the funds eight years later and founded the Smithsonian Institution. Joseph Henry, the first secretary of the Smithsonian, committed the institution to studies in linguistics, archaeology, and ethnology. The original building (commonly known as The Castle, which today houses the administrative offices of the institution's numerous museums, galleries, gardens, and the National Zoo) was built in 1855. In 1879, the institution established the Bureau of Ethnology under the direction of John Wesley Powell. Collections from archaeological studies in the eastern half of the country and the ethnological material collected during the four U.S. Geological Surveys placed a burden on the facilities of the institution. In 1881, Congress funded the building of the National Museum to be under the administration of the Smithsonian to house and to exhibit the collections to the public.
8. Stevenson, *Scrapbook a*, 11.
9. For a biography "that is the history not of a personality but of a career," see Stegner, *Beyond the Hundredth Meridian. John Wesley Powell and the Second Opening of the West*. For more specific focus on Powell's work within the Bureau of Ethnology, see Hinsley, *Savages and Scientists*.

10. For more extensive information about collecting by the National Museum during this period, see Parezo, "The Formation of Ethnographic Collections."

11. Stevenson, "Illustrated Catalogue."

12. Smithsonian Institution, *Bureau of Ethnology,* "Annual Report of the Director 1881–1882," XX–XXI.

13. A study of early maps and photographs indicates that the wagon road must have reached the top of the mesa a short distance north of the foot-trail, circled around behind the Corn clan and Tobacco clan rooms, and entered the plaza of Hano from the west side of the mesa. References hereinafter to the "trail" apply to either the footpath or the wagon road.

14. Victor Mindeleff, "A Study of Pueblo Architecture, Tusayan and Cibola," 61. The "American" is not identified.

15. See McClusky, "Evangelists, Educators, Ethnographers, and the Establishment of the Hopi Reservation" for the conclusive reason for the decision to create a Hopi reservation.

16. U.S. Congress. Senate. *Indian Affairs, Laws and Treaties. Vol. 1.*

17. Riordan to the commissioner of Indian affairs, July 3, 1883. National Archives, Laguna Niguel. Record Group 75.

18. Victor Mindeleff, "A Study of Pueblo Architecture, Tusayan and Cibola."

19. Joseph Stanley-Brown to FHC, Oct. 30, 1882. Green, *Cushing at Zuni,* 247.

20. For a first-hand report of the Oraibi incident, see Cushing, "Contributions to Hopi History." See also Hinsley, "Collecting Cultures and Cultures of Collecting."

21. Smithsonian Institution, *Bureau of Ethnology,* "Annual Report of the Director 1882–83, XL."

22. Ibid.

23. Smithsonian Institution, *Bureau of Ethnology,* "Annual Report of the Director 1885–86," XXIV–XXV.

24. Stevenson, *Scrapbook a,* 20.

25. Ibid., 21.

26. Ibid., page following 32, unnumbered.

27. Holmes, "Pottery of the Ancient Pueblos," 321.

28. Stevenson, *Scrapbook a,* page following 32, unnumbered.

Chapter 4. Schools

1. If only a good biography of Tom Polacca were possible! Only references to him can be found in journals and reports. When Polacca was hired at $1.00 per day to act as interpreter and guide for Frank Hamilton Cushing on an expedition to Havasupai in 1881, he gave Cushing a "long account of his wanderings to California. The ocean, people, steamboats, porpoises, *and* dolphins, sea shells, printing, book stores, street cars, wheat and fruits, etc. etc. A good observer, and description wonderfully realistic." (Green, *Cushing at Zuni,* 168.) Another evening on the trip, "Pu-la-ka-kai tells of printing, distribution of mail, fountains, his dancing, his presents, the friends he made, animals of the ocean steamers, Americans who spoke a different language, a museum, graftings, Chinese store, silk, ribbands, lacquer-ware, houses of prostitution—Talk with captain of steamer, landing of passengers" (Ibid., 169).

Artist Willard Metcalf, who accompanied Cushing and Mindeleff "to clean out Oraibi" in 1882, described Polacca as "a believer in Americans, has very advanced and common-sense ideas in certain matters, wore American clothes and was quite wealthy . . . a great linguist, speaking no less than six or seven Indian languages, most of them perfectly, and also Spanish and English" (Ibid., 257).

One can speculate on how an otherwise traditional Hopi-Tewa family could produce two such remarkable individuals as brother and sister, Tom Polacca and Nampeyo.

2. The jewelry room of the present Keams Canyon Trading Post is the structure that Thomas Keam built on the wagon road after selling his first post and property to the federal government in 1887. The present inner wall surface of plywood was nailed to the frame that held the original sheet metal. Over the years, an entrance vestibule, restaurant, and rug room have been added to the original building, and a grocery/general merchandise store with a separate entrance has been built adjacent to it. Keam's residence still stands on the knoll opposite the post at the entrance to the box canyon.

3. U.S. Bureau of the Census, *Eleventh Census, Extra Census Bulletin,* 59.

4. Vandever to Prince, September 8, 1890. New Mexico Archives, Santa Fe.

5. U.S. Bureau of the Census, *Eleventh Census, Extra Census Bulletin* (McCook report for 1890–1891), 36–37.

6. Keam to Commissioner Morgan, February 14, 1890. Quoted in Yava, *Big Falling Snow,* 157.

7. Keam to Commissioner Morgan, January 13, 1890. Ibid., 156.

8. "Conference with Moqui Pueblos," June 27, 1890. Ibid., 161–64.

9. H. C. Corbin, assistant adjutant general, to the commanding general, Department of Arizona, July 2, 1891. U.S. Bureau of the Census, *Eleventh Census, Extra Census Bulletin,* 37.

Chapter 5. Two Anthropologists

1. The little that is known about Alexander M. Stephen's life and a discussion of the two catalogs that he compiled about pottery in the Thomas V. Keam Collection of Material Culture are included in the introduction to *Hopi Pottery Symbols* by Alex Patterson.

2. Stephen, *Hopi Journal of Alexander M. Stephen,* 882.

3. Ibid., 385.

4. Ibid., 940.

5. Ibid.

6. Ibid., 481–83.

7. Ibid., 130.

8. No definitive biography of Jesse Walter Fewkes has been published at this date. A small booklet compiled by Mrs. F. S. Nichols entitled *Biography and Bibliography of Jesse Walter Fewkes* (no date) was privately printed. Walter Hough wrote two biographical essays after Fewkes's death: "Jesse Walter Fewkes" and "Biographical Memoir of Jesse Walter Fewkes 1850–1930."

9. Fewkes to Hemenway, July 2, 1891. Quoted in Wade, *America's Great Lost Expedition,* 5–6.

10. Ibid.

11. Ibid.

12. Fewkes, "Contributions to Hopi History," 277.

13. Fewkes, "Tusayan Katcinas."

14. Ibid., 277.

15. Stephen, *Hopi Journal,* 198.

16. Ibid., 201.

17. Related by a descendant of Nampeyo. December 13, 1988.

18. Stephen, *Hopi Journal,* 861.

19. Ibid., 862.

20. Fewkes, "Tusayan Migration Traditions," 578.

21. Wade and McChesney, *America's Great Lost Expedition* and *Historic Hopi Ceramics.*

Chapter 6. Sikyatki and the Snake Dance

1. U.S. Bureau of the Census, *Eleventh Census, Extra Census Bulletin,* 6.

2. Hodge, Notebook of the Sikyatki Excavation. Tuesday, July 24, 1895.

3. Mrs. Hodge's drawings illustrated Fewkes's article "Archeological Expedition to Arizona in 1895."

4. Fewkes, "Preliminary Account of an Expedition to the Cliff Villages of Red Rock Country and the Tusayan Ruins of Sikyatki and Awatobi, Arizona, in 1895."

5. Fewkes, "Archeological Expedition to Arizona in 1895."

6. Fewkes, "Preliminary Account," 557.

7. Hodge, Notebook, Sunday, July 28, 1895.

8. Fewkes, "Archeological Expedition," 635.

9. Hodge, Notebook, Saturday, July 27, 1895.

10. In his annual report for 1895, Director Powell of the Bureau of Ethnology stated that seventeen boxes of ceramics had been excavated from Sikyatki and Awatovi and three from the headwaters of the Rio Verde. XXXIX.

11. Harrison, "First Mention in Print of the Hopi Snake Dance."

12. Stevenson, *Scrapbook a,* 34.

13. Bourke, *Snake Dance of the Moquis of Arizona,* 1.

14. Bourke, *Snake Dance.*

15. McNitt, *Richard Wetherill: Anasazi,* 89.

16. Ibid.

17. Fewkes, "Preliminary Account," 577.

18. Fewkes, "Archeological Expedition," 632 n. 1.

19. Ibid., 660.

Chapter 7. Missionaries

1. Mary-Russell F. and Harold S. Colton added another erroneous element to the Sikyatki story in their article "An Appreciation of the Art of Nampeyo and Her Influence on Hopi Pottery" (*Plateau,* 15(3):92). They stated that

Walter Hough had assisted Fewkes during the excavation of Sikyatki and, in his article "A Revival of Ancient Hopi Pottery Art," had described Nampeyo's visits to the site to copy pottery designs. The Coltons misread Hough's account. Hough accompanied Fewkes to excavate old Shongopovi in 1896 but was not present at Sikyatki in 1895.

2. Fewkes, "Archeological Expedition," 592 n. 1.
3. Hough, "A Revival of the Ancient Hopi Pottery Art," 322.
4. Hough, *The Hopi Indians*, 76.
5. Ibid., 75.
6. The bowls are in the collection of the National Museum of Natural History, Smithsonian Institution, Washington D.C. Although the collection was made by Walter Hough, the name "J. W. Fewkes" is printed on the bottom of each bowl.
7. The purpose of the ceremony, held late in November or early December, is the blessing of new houses in the pueblo. Six men in huge, birdlike costumes perform the rites, followed by all-night festivities and a race by the Shalakos the following day.
8. Yava, *Big Falling Snow*, 13.
9. Fewkes to Hodge, January 2, 1898. Hodge Collection.
10. Nequatewa, "Dr. Fewkes and Masauwu."
11. Little, *Jacob Hamblin, A Narrative of His Personal Experience as a Frontiersman, Missionary to the Indians, and Explorer*, 58.
12. Wright, *Hopi Material Culture*, 2.
13. When Harold Colton assigned Nequatewa to prepare a short biographical article about Nampeyo after her death, Colton wrote to Herman Schweizer of the Fred Harvey Company requesting any information Schweizer might be able to contribute. Schweizer at that time was old and ill. On October 31, 1942, Schweizer replied to Colton's query:

> I remember her very well. My first contact with her was in 1898 when we made an exhibit in the Coliseum in Chicago for The Santa Fe Railway, and we brought Nampeyo and her husband, Layso, to Chicago . . . through the good offices of Dr. Dorsey, then Curator of the Department of Anthropology in the Field Museum, who in turn handled the

detail with a missionary named Voth who did a lot of altars for the Field Museum.

In a letter dated November 12, Colton questioned Schweizer further:

> Edmund Nequatewa learned from her family that in 1910 she went to Chicago to demonstrate at some exposition, along with other Hopis, which included her cousin Vivian from Second Mesa [This information is incorrect. Nellie and Ida Avayo accompanied Nampeyo and Lesso.] . . . You said in your letter to me that she demonstrated eleven years earlier at the Colloseum [*sic*] at a Santa Fe Railroad exhibition. Was this another exposition of the same sort?

Schweizer answered on December 31, after returning from the hospital:

> The information about Edmund is correct. The Exposition in Chicago was in the Colloseum [*sic*]. For several years they had exhibits in the Colloseum called Sportsmen's Show where they exhibited all kind of sporting goods of different firms, such as fishing tackle, guns, rifles, knives, and what not, and the Santa Fe was asked to participate.

This reply must have confused Colton, but without confirming the information, he inserted a handwritten paragraph into Nequatewa's original typed and edited manuscript entitled "Nampeyo, Famous Hopi Potter" that, upon publication, read:

> In 1898 through the efforts of Dr. G. A. Dorsey, then Curator of Anthropology at the Field Museum, and a missionary, H. R. Voth, the Santa Fe Railroad brought Nampeyo and her husband Lesou to Chicago, to make pottery at a Santa Fe Railway Exhibition held in the Coliseum.

(All quoted references above are from the Colton Collection.) Research at the Chicago Historical Society produced no reference to either a Santa Fe Railway Exhibition or Sportsmen's Show held in 1898 at the Coliseum. No information regarding the exhibition or Dorsey's or Voth's involvement with such an exhibition has been found at the Field Museum, the Newberry Library in Chicago, or the Mennonite Library and Archives in Kansas. Records of the Santa Fe Railway were destroyed at the turn of the century, but some records of the railway in the collection of the Kansas State Historical Society yielded no information. Inquiries to the Orvis Company, Colt Industries, and the American Museum of Fly Fishing produced no record of a Sportsmen's Show in 1898. Navajo Agency and Moqui Agency records were checked, but no record of permission for Nampeyo to travel off the reservation was found. A Trans-Mississippi and International Exposition was held in Omaha, Nebraska, in 1898, but the agent in charge of recruiting pueblo Indians from New Mexico and Arizona sent twenty men, all from Santa Clara Pueblo in New Mexico. Fred Harvey's papers have been scattered, and Schweizer's own files could not be located. However, Herman Schweizer apparently began work as a news agent for Fred Harvey in 1899. (Harvey, *The Fred Harvey Company Collects Indian Art*, 1.)

14. Yava, *Big Falling Snow*, 136.

15. Author's conversation with a Mormon missionary who wishes to remain anonymous, July 20, 1986.

16. Barker, "Intrepid Indian Elder," 13.

17. Yava, *Big Falling Snow*, 11.

18. Author's conversation with a Mormon missionary who wishes to remain anonymous, July 20, 1986. The story was confirmed by one of Tom Polacca's granddaughters.

19. Although Polacca traveled widely for the purpose of trading, he did not own or operate a trading post. This was confirmed by Byron Hunter, current manager of the gift shop at the Heard Museum, who had worked many years in a trading post in Polacca. The post, a branch of the Keams Canyon Trading Post owned by the McGee family, burned to the ground in 1968. Conversation with the author, January 19, 1987.

20. Smith, "Tom Pavatea, Hopi Trader," 6.

Chapter 8. Making a Pot

1. Stephen, *Hopi Journal*, 1188.

2. Hough, *The Hopi Indians*, 78.

3. Stephen, *Hopi Journal*, 1189.

4. Kate Cory's diary is in the collection of the Smoki Museum, Prescott, Arizona; a typed transcript is in the collection of the Museum of Northern Arizona, Flagstaff. Many of her photos were reproduced in *The Hopi Photographs, Kate Cory: 1905–1912* by Marnie and Marc Gaede. Surprisingly, even though Cory's diary contains a few disjointed references to Nampeyo, she took no photographs of the potter. The photo archivist of the Museum of Northern Arizona, which holds the Cory photograph collection, did not find a listing of any photo identified as Nampeyo and, checking the contact prints, found only one photo of a potter, who was not Nampeyo. (Dorothy A. House, Librarian, Museum of Northern Arizona, to the author, September 4, 1987.)

5. Cory Diary, 55.

6. Stephen, *Hopi Journal*, 482.

7. Barrett, "Pottery," 21.

8. The photograph by Sumner Matteson of Nampeyo and Annie (who was misidentified as Nellie in the text *Side Trips, The Photography of Sumner W. Matteson 1898–1908* by Louis B. Casagrande and Phillips Bourns) was presumptively dated 1901 by the authors. When I asked two members of Nampeyo's family to compare Matteson's photograph with those known to have been taken in 1901 by A. C. Vroman, both said that Matteson's was taken several years earlier, that Annie was much younger in Matteson's photograph. I discussed their assertions with co-author Bourns, who said that Matteson may have taken the photo between 1895 and 1899, a period during which Bourns cannot account for Matteson's travels. If, during further research, he finds that Matteson visited First Mesa before 1900, the photograph will be the earliest to picture jars made by Nampeyo. (See Chapter 17, Stylistic Analysis of Vessels, Period 1, for more discussion about the photograph.)

9. See Chapter 17, Stylistic Analysis of Vessels, for more discussion about collaboration between Nampeyo and her family.

Chapter 9. Photographers and Collectors

1. For more information about the commodification of the American Indian during the latter half of the nineteenth and the early twentieth centuries, see Hinsley, "The World as a Marketplace" and "Collecting Cultures and Cultures of Collecting."
2. Vroman's collection is in the Southwest Museum, Los Angeles.
3. See Notes, Chapter 8, no. 8.
4. George H. Pepper's collection is in the Middle American Research Institute, Tulane University, New Orleans. Nineteen of the twenty-two vessels remain in the collection.
5. Dorsey, *Indians of the Southwest*, 139.
6. Ibid., 108.
7. Virginia Walker Couse to Frances Walker Kamm, n.d. Couse Family Collection.
8. Couse Family Collection.
9. Mary Coulter's collection is in the museum at Mesa Verde National Park, Colorado.
10. Ole Solberg's collection is in the Ethnographic Museum, University of Oslo, Norway.
11. Burbank and Royce, *Burbank among the Indians*, 73.
12. Burbank's drawing of Nampeyo hangs above the doorway to the first left bedroom in Hubbell's ranch house, Hubbell Trading Post, Ganado.
13. Many of Jo Mora's paintings and photographs were published in *The Year of the Hopi, Paintings and Photographs by Joseph Mora, 1904–1906*.
14. Mora's painting of the red trading post is in the collection of the Hubbell Trading Post National Historic Site, Ganado.
15. Pamphlet "Catalogue and Price List, Navajo Blankets & Indian Curios, J. L. Hubbell, Indian Trader," 2. Southwest Museum.
16. Ibid., 13.
17. The Hubbell Trading Post and ranch house are now designated a National Historic Site under the administration of the Department of the Interior. The post is still actively used by neighboring Navajos.
18. For a history of the Fred Harvey Company, see Poling-Kempes, *The Harvey Girls*. More specifically focused on the relationship between the Fred Harvey Company and the Santa Fe Railway are Dilworth, *Imagining the Primitive* and Weigle, "From Desert to Disney World: The Santa Fe Railway and the Fred Harvey Company Display the Indian Southwest."
19. By 1906, Hopi pottery had become so popular that Theo. Y. Lemmon, Superintendent of the Moqui School in Keams Canyon, received a letter from Miss Josephine Foord, a representative of the Commissioner of Indian Affairs working in Laguna Pueblo, New Mexico. Her duties were "to travel and improve the pottery" at pueblos suggested by the commissioner. In the letter, Foord asked Lemmon to purchase some Hopi pottery that could be glazed and fired for exhibition and sale. Lemmon felt that such an idea would "not meet the approval of present traders in this section. I am, too, of the opinion that as soon as Hopi pottery becomes something beside Hopi pottery it is not worth shelf room. . . . As half Hopi and half something else it is at best, in my judgment, a halfbreed of the worst sort." (Letter from Theo Y. Lemmon, superintendent, to the commissioner of Indian affairs, Washington, D.C., September 12, 1906. U.S. Department of the Interior, correspondence from superintendent of Moqui Training School and Moqui Agency, Hopi Agency, Keams Canyon.)

Chapter 10. Hopi House

1. For a well illustrated account of the Santa Fe Railway's advertising campaign, see *Dream Tracks* by T. C. McLuhan.
2. Huckel to Schweizer, January 24, 1907. Hubbell Collection.
3. Huckel to Hubbell, September 30, 1905. Ibid.
4. Schweizer to Hubbell, January 5, 1907. Ibid.
5. Schweizer to Hubbell, January 22, 1907. Ibid.
6. Author's conversation with Jo Mora, Jr., June 3, 1988.
7. Huckel to Hubbell, January 7, 1905. Hubbell Collection.
8. Huckel to Hubbell, March 26, 1905. Ibid.
9. *El Tovar: A New Hotel at Grand Canyon of Arizona*, N.d.
10. *Hotel El Tovar: On the Rim of the Grand Canyon*, 1909.
11. Huckel to Hubbell, December 7, 1906. Hubbell Collection.

12. Edmund Nequatewa was born on Second Mesa about 1880 and lived with his wife and three sons in Shipolovi. After two of his sons died at the Phoenix Indian School, he and his wife moved to Flagstaff so the remaining son could attend public school. He was hired by the Museum of Northern Arizona as a maintenance man and liaison with the Hopi people. After Nampeyo's death, Harold S. Colton of the museum sent Nequatewa to First Mesa to gather biographical information about the potter, which was published under Nequatewa's by-line and entitled "Nampeyo, Famous Hopi Potter." Certain "transgressions" later led to Nequatewa's dismissal from the museum (Seaman, *Born A Chief*, xxiii). He subsequently remarried, moved to Hotevilla on Third Mesa, and became associated with a Protestant religious sect. He died in Hotevilla on April 28, 1969.

13. Nequatea, undated manuscript entitled "Nampeyo." Colton Collection.

Chapter 11. Children

1. Hough, "Archeological Field Work in Northeastern Arizona," 357.
2. Yava, *Big Falling Snow*, 115.

Chapter 12. Chicago

1. Schweizer to Hubbell, May 12, 1906. Hubbell Collection.
2. Huckel to Hubbell, September 30, 1905. Ibid.
3. Ibid.
4. Huckel to Hubbell, December 2, 1905. Ibid.
5. Huckel to Hubbell, December 11, 1905. Ibid.
6. Schweizer to Hubbell, February 6, 1907. Ibid. The "wheel girl" is not identified.
7. Schweizer to Hubbell, April 5, 1908. Ibid.
8. Schweizer to Hubbell, February 20, 1908. Ibid.
9. Miller to Schweizer, January 25, 1910. Ibid.
10. Miller to Schweizer, August 9, 1910. U.S. Department of the Interior correspondence, Hopi Agency.
11. Quoted in Miller to Drummond, October 28, 1910. Ibid.
12. "Land Show Is On," unnumbered page following page 1.
13. Ibid., 1 and following page.
14. Letters relating to the Land Show in U.S. Department of the Interior correspondence, Hopi

Agency, do not indicate when the family returned from Chicago.
15. Miller, "To Whom Presented," September 6, 1910. U.S. Department of the Interior correspondence, Hopi Agency.
16. The birthdate "1853" may have been given to the church by descendants. The birthdate of 1849 used by the author was that given by Polacca to Sarah Abbott for the 1900 federal census.
17. E. S. Clark, Special Enumerator, U.S. Bureau of the Census, *Eleventh Census, Extra Census Bulletin. 50.*

Chapter 13. Published Distortions

1. Barrett's collection is on permanent exhibit in the Milwaukee Public Museum.
2. Leigh's collection is in the Gilcrease Museum, Tulsa.
3. A bronze casting of the portrait is in the collection of the Heard Museum.
4. Kopta's widow, Anna, donated his photographs of Hopi ceremonies to the Museum of the American Indian, New York, and his photographs of daily life and activities to the Museum of Northern Arizona, Flagstaff. Many of the latter photographs were reproduced in *Hopi Scenes of Everyday Life. Plateau.*
5. Freire-Marreco, "Tewa Kinship Terms from the Pueblo of Hano, Arizona," 285.
6. Schmedding, *Cowboy and Indian Trader*, 314–15.
7. Ibid., 338–39.
8. Crane, *Indians of the Enchanted Desert*, 179.
9. Ibid., 238.
10. Ibid., 255.
11. Fewkes, "Designs on Prehistoric Hopi Pottery."
12. Ibid., 218.
13. Ibid., 279.
14. After Nequatewa's manuscript for the article "Nampeyo, Famous Hopi Potter" had gone to the printer but before publication in January of 1943, Harold S. Colton contradicted the assertion in the article that the revival of Hopi pottery had begun in 1895 when Jesse Walter Fewkes excavated Sikyatki. In a letter to Dr. M. W. Stirling, Smithsonian Institution, dated December 2, 1942, Colton stated, "Also he [Nequatewa] found that [Nampeyo] was using prehistoric designs as as [sic] inspiration for her

pottery before Fewkes' excavation at Sikyatki in 1895. (Stephens [sic]—*Hopi Journal*, December 1892.)" Colton Collection. Unfortunately, his correction was not incorporated into the published article.

15. For a background of Hewett and his work in the Southwest, see Elliott, *The School of American Research. A History: The First Eighty Years.* Also see Chauvenet, *Hewett and Friends.*

16. Hough, "A Revival of the Ancient Hopi Pottery Art," 322.

17. Hodge, Notebook of the Sikyatki Excavation.

Chapter 14. Diminishing Sight

1. Crane, *Indians of the Enchanted Desert*, 228.

2. Judd, "Nampeyo, An Additional Note," 92.

3. Frisbie, "The Influence of J. Walter Fewkes on Nampeyo: Fact or Fancy?" 236.

4. Bunzel, *The Pueblo Potter.*

5. Carl Oscar Borg's notebook of poems. Collection of Helen Laird.

6. Bunzel, *The Pueblo Potter*, 68.

7. Ibid., 42.

8. Related by Daisy Hooee, December 10, 1987.

9. James, *Pages from Hopi History*, 184. James, an activist for the welfare of the American Indian, devoted an entire chapter in *Pages* to the "Oppression by Superintendent Daniel," 176–84.

10. Author's conversation with Anna Kopta, widow of Emry Kopta, November 7, 1985.

Chapter 15. Alone

1. The piece is described as "effigy container; man w/painted vest (?); man sitting on cylindrical object; man's body hollow; ht. 9.5 cm." and "tourist piece, made for sale." Cat. #2-47043.

2. Bunzel, *The Pueblo Potter*, 68.

3. Ibid., 7.

4. Ibid., 68.

5. The Melvilles' collection is at Wesleyan University and is illustrated in Walker and Wyckoff, *Hopis, Tewas and the American Road.*

6. Allen, *Contemporary Hopi Pottery*, 69.

Chapter 16. Death

1. Burbank and Royce, *Burbank among the Indians*, 222.

2. The federal government funded projects to stabilize houses, repair roofs, and add floors and some bathrooms in Walpi in the late 1970s and in Hano in the early 1980s. Archaeological studies were made in the villages at the time, and the uncovered artifacts were placed in trust for the people.

3. Bunzel, *The Pueblo Potter*, 65.

4. Author's conversation with Anna Kopta, widow of Emry Kopta, November 7, 1985.

5. Author's conversation with Margaret Tafoya, August 20, 1988.

6. Tad Nichols described a field trip he had taken as a student at the University of Arizona in 1935. It was August and hot, and he remembers pushing cars through mud to get to the mesas. The students walked through the plaza at Hano and found Nampeyo seated outside her house with a display of pots. She looked very old but was not completely blind. Her gnarled hands made a little pot for the students while they watched and she posed for photographs (Photgraph 25). Author's conversation with Nichols, March 11, 1987.

7. Douma to Maurine Grammer, July 21, 1939. Collection of Maurine Grammer.

8. Nampeyo's stone house on the mesa has been replaced by a cinder-block house, and the government-built house in Polacca is no longer standing.

9. Hodge, "Death of Nampeyo," 164.

10. "The Age of Nampeyo the Potter." *Masterkey* 16(6):223.

11. Stirling to Colton, October [date illegible], 1942. Colton Collection.

12. *Plateau* 15(3):40–42.

13. See Borg's poem "Nam-Pey-O," Chapter 14.

14. Author's conversation with Byron Hunter, January 19, 1987.

15. *Arizona Women's Hall of Fame*, Arizona Historical Society, Museum Monograph, 1986.

Chapter 17. Stylistic Analysis of Vessels

1. One authorized excavation of Awatovi has been made more recently. See Smith, *Painted Ceramics of the Western Mound at Awatovi.*

2. Leigh's collection is in the Gilcrease Museum.

3. Pepper's collection is in the Middle American Research Institute, Tulane University, New Orleans.

4. Bunzel, *The Pueblo Potter.*

5. State of Arizona, certified copy of vital record for Lesso. Date of death, May 7, 1930.

6. See Notes, Chapter 8, no. 8.

7. Hubert, "An Introduction to Hopi Pottery Design," 82.

8. In his original manuscript, *Pottery of Tusayan: Catalogue of the Keam Collection* (National Anthropological Archives, Smithsonian Institution, Washington D.C.), Alexander M. Stephen described the meanings of symbols on ancient Hopi pottery. The catalog has been reprinted in its entirety in Patterson, *Hopi Pottery Symbols*. In his introduction, Patterson warns, however, that the meaning of the symbols told to Stephen in 1890 may not have had the same meaning to potters centuries earlier.

9. Bunzel, *The Pueblo Potter*, 68.

10. Ibid.

11. Ibid., 42.

12. State of Arizona, certified copy of vital record for Lesso.

13. Author's conversation with Anna Kopta, widow of Emry Kopta, November 7, 1985.

14. Stephen, *Hopi Journal*, 130.

15. Colton, "Pottery Types of the Southwest." Ware 7B—Types 20 and 21. No page number.

Bibliography

The following references are cited because of their significant background and historical information or because of their direct relationship to the subject. The reader should be aware that many of them include the biographical fallacies about Nampeyo and her pottery that are enumerated in Appendix A of this text. The author has excluded those articles and essays that merely repeat erroneous "common knowledge" about the potter without offering new or original research.

Adams, E. Charles. 1979. *Walpi Archaeological Project Phase II*. Vols. 1, 3. Flagstaff: Museum of Northern Arizona.

"The Age of Nampeyo The Potter." *Masterkey* 16(6):223.

Allen, Laura Graves. 1984. *Contemporary Hopi Pottery*. Flagstaff: Museum of Northern Arizona.

Bailey, Garrick, and Roberta Glenn. 1986. *A History of the Navajos, The Reservation Years*. Santa Fe: School of American Research Press.

Barker, Clarence S. "Intrepid Indian Elder, Wife Help Convert Neighbors." *Deseret News*. September 27, 1950, 13. Historical Department, Church of Jesus Christ of Latter-day Saints, Salt Lake City.

Barrett, Samuel. 1911. "Pottery." Manuscript. Samuel Barrett Papers. Bancroft Library, University of California, Berkeley.

Bourke, John G. 1884. *Snake Dance of the Moquis of Arizona*. New York: Charles Scribner's Sons.

Reprint, 1984. Tucson: University of Arizona Press.

Brand, Donald D., and Fred E. Harvey, eds. 1939. *So Live the Works of Men. Seventieth Anniversary Volume Honoring Edgar Lee Hewett*. Albuquerque: University of New Mexico Press.

Brew, J.O. 1979. "Hopi Prehistory and History to 1850." In *Handbook of North American Indians. Southwest, Vol. 9*, 514–23. Washington, D.C.: Smithsonian Institution.

Brophy, William A., and Sophie D. Aberle, comps. 1966. *The Indian Report of the Commission on the Rights, Liberties, and Responsibilities of the American Indian*. Norman: University of Oklahoma Press.

Brushstrokes on the Plateau. Plateau. 56(1). Museum of Northern Arizona.

Bunzel, Ruth. 1929. *The Pueblo Potter*. New York: Columbia University Press. Reprint, 1972. New York: Dover Publications.

Burbank, E.A., and Ernest Royce. 1946. *Burbank among the Indians*. Caldwell, Idaho: Caxton Printers.

Casagrande, Louis B., and Phillips Bourns. 1983. *Side Trips, The Photography of Sumner W. Matteson 1898–1908*. Milwaukee Public Museum and Science Museum of Minnesota.

Chauvenet, Beatrice. 1983. *Hewett and Friends*. Santa Fe: Museum of New Mexico Press.

Colton Collection. Museum of Northern Arizona, Flagstaff.

Colton, Harold S., ed. 1950. *Pottery Types of the*

Southwest. Museum of Northern Arizona Ceramic Series, no. 3C. Flagstaff: Northern Arizona Society of Science and Art.

Cory, Kate. Diary. Smoki Museum, Prescott, Arizona. Photocopy of typed transcription, Museum of Northern Arizona Library.

Courlander, Harold. 1971. *The Fourth World of the Hopis.* New York: Crown Publishers. Reprint, 1987. Albuquerque: University of New Mexico Press.

——— 1982. *Hopi Voices.* Albuquerque: University of New Mexico Press.

Crane, Leo. 1925. *Indians of the Enchanted Desert.* Boston: Little Brown and Company. Reprint, 1972. Glorieta, N.M.: Rio Grande Press.

Current, Karen. 1978. *Photography and the Old West.* New York: Harry N. Abrams and Amon Carter Museum of Western Art.

Curtis, Edward S. 1922. *The North American Indian, 12th Vol., The Hopi.* Norwood: Plimpton Press.

Curtis, Natalie. 1923. *The Indians Book.* New York: Harper Brothers.

Cushing, Frank Hamilton. 1922. "Contributions to Hopi History; I. Oraibi in 1883." *American Anthropologist* 24(3):253–68.

Davis, Barbara A. 1985. *Edward S. Curtis, The Life and Times of a Shadow Catcher.* San Francisco: Chronicle Books.

Dilworth, Leah Collett. 1995. *Imagining the Primitive: Representations of Native Americans in the Southwest, 1880–1930.* Ann Arbor: U.M.I. Dissertation Services.

Dockstader, Frederick J. 1979. "Hopi History, 1850–1940." In *Handbook of North American Indians. Southwest, Vol. 9,* 524–32. Washington, D.C.: Smithsonian Institution.

Dorsey, George A. 1903. *Indians of the Southwest.* Passenger Department, Atchison, Topeka and Santa Fe Railway System.

Dozier, Edward P. 1966. *Hano: A Tewa Indian Community in Arizona.* New York: Holt, Rinehart, and Winston.

El Tovar Hotel pamphlets:

——— n.d. *El Tovar, A New Hotel at Grand Canyon of Arizona.* Text by W.H. Simpson.

——— 1909. *Hotel El Tovar on the Rim of the Grand Canyon.* Management of Fred Harvey.

Elliot, Malinda. 1987. *The School of American Research. A History: The First Eighty Years.* Santa Fe: School of American Research.

Fewkes, Jesse Walter. 1896. "Preliminary Account of an Expedition to the Cliff Villages of Red Rock Country and the Tusayan Ruins of Sikyatki and Awatobi, Arizona, in 1895." In *Smithsonian Institution Annual Report 1895,* 557–88. Washington, D.C.

——— 1897. "Tusayan Katcinas." In *Bureau of Ethnology 15th Annual Report 1893–94,* 245–313. Washington, D.C.

——— 1898. "Archeological Expedition into Arizona in 1895." In *Bureau of American Ethnology 17th Annual Report 1895–96,* 519–742. Washington, D.C.

——— 1900. "Tusayan Migration Traditions." In *Bureau of American Ethnology 19th Annual Report 1897–98,* 573–633. Washington, D.C.

——— 1919. "Designs on Prehistoric Hopi Pottery." In *Bureau of American Ethnology 33rd Annual Report 1911–12,* 207–84. Washington, D.C.

——— 1922. "Contributions to Hopi History; II. Oraibi in 1890." *American Anthropologist* 24(3):268–83.

Fred Harvey Fine Arts Collection. 1976. Phoenix: Heard Museum.

Freire-Marreco, Barbara. 1914. "Tewa Kinship Terms from the Pueblo of Hano, Arizona." *American Anthropologist* 16(2):269–87.

Frigout, Arlette. 1979. "Hopi Ceremonial Organization." In *Handbook of North American Indians. Southwest, Vol. 9,* 564–76. Washington, D.C.: Smithsonian Institution.

Frisbie, Theodore R. 1973. "The Influence of J. Walter Fewkes on Nampeyo: Fact or Fancy?" In *The Changing Ways of Southwestern Indians, A Historic Perspective,* Ed. Albert H. Schroeder, 231–44. Glorieta, N.M.: Rio Grande Press.

Foresee, Aylesa. 1964. *William Henry Jackson, Pioneer Photographer of the West.* New York: Viking Press.

Gaede, Marnie and Marc. 1986. *The Hopi Photographs, Kate Cory: 1905–1912.* La Cañada, Calif.: Chaco Press.

Grattan, Virginia L. 1980. *Mary Colter, Builder upon the Red Earth.* Flagstaff: Northland Press.

Graves, Laura L. 1992. *Thomas Varker Keam. The Biography of a Nineteenth Century Indian Trader in Northeast Arizona.* Ann Arbor; U.M.I. Dissertation Services.

Green, Jesse, ed. 1990. *Cushing at Zuni. The Cor-*

respondence and Journals of Frank Hamilton Cushing 1879–1884. Albuquerque: University of New Mexico Press.

Harlow, Francis H. 1977. Modern Pueblo Pottery 1880–1960. Flagstaff: Northland Press.

Harlow, Francis H., and Larry Frank 1974. Historic Pottery of the Pueblo Indians. Boston: New York Graphic Society.

Harrison, Michael. 1964, "First Mention in Print of the Hopi Snake Dance." Masterkey 8(4): 150–55.

Harvey, Byron. 1981. The Fred Harvey Company Collects Indian Art. Phoenix: Heard Museum.

Hays, Kelley Ann, and Diane Dittemore. 1990. "Seven Centuries of Hopi Pottery: Yellow Ware from Arizona State Museum Collections." American Indian Art 15(3):56–65.

Hinsley, Curtis. 1981. Savages and Scientists: The Smithsonian Institution and the Development of American Anthropology 1846-1910. Washington, D.C.: Smithsonian Institution Press.

——— 1983. "Ethnographic Charisma and Scientific Routine." In History of Anthropology: Observers Observed. Vol 1. Madison: University of Wisconsin Press.

——— 1991. "The World as a Marketplace: Commodification of the Exotic at the World's Columbian Exposition, Chicago, 1893." In Exhibiting Cultures. The Politics of Museum Display, 344–71. Washington, D.C.: Smithsonian Institution Press.

——— 1992. "Collecting Cultures and Cultures of Collecting: The Lure of the American Southwest 1880–1915." Museum Anthropology 16(1)12–20.

Hodge Collection. Southwest Museum, Los Angeles.

Hodge, Frederick Webb. 1895. Notebook of the Sikyatki Excavation. Southwest Museum, Los Angeles.

——— 1942. "Death of Nampeyo." Masterkey 16(5):164.

Holmes, William Henry. 1886. "Pottery of the Ancient Pueblos." In Bureau of Ethnology 4th Annual Report 1882–83, 257–521. Washington, D.C.

Hopi and Hopi-Tewa Pottery. Plateau. 49(3). Museum of Northern Arizona.

Hopi Scenes of Everyday Life. Plateau. 55(1). Museum of Northern Arizona.

Hough, Walter. 1903. "Archeological Field Work in Northeastern Arizona; The Museum-Gates Expedition of 1901." In U.S. National Museum Report 1901, 279–358. Washington, D.C.

——— 1915. The Hopi Indians. Cedar Rapids: Torch Press.

——— 1917. "A Revival of the Ancient Hopi Pottery Art." American Anthropologist 19(2): 322–23.

——— 1931. "Jesse Walter Fewkes." American Anthropologist 33(1):92–97.

——— 1932. "Biographical Memoir of Jesse Walter Fewkes 1850–1930." In National Academy of Sciences Biographical Memoirs. Vol 15. Ninth Memoir, 261–83. Washington, D.C.: National Academy of Sciences.

Hubbell Papers. University of Arizona Library, Special Collections, Tucson.

Hubert, Virgil. 1937. "Introduction to Hopi Pottery Design." Museum Notes, Museum of Northern Arizona 10(1):80–87.

Hurst, Tricia. 1982. "Emry Kopta, Each Respected the Other." Southwest Art 11(11):84–91.

Jackson, William Henry. 1929. The Pioneer Photographer: Rocky Mountain Adventures with a Camera. Yonkers-on-Hudson, N.Y.: World Book.

——— 1940. Time Exposure: The Autobiography of William Henry Jackson. New York: G.P. Putnam's Sons.

James, Harry C. 1974. Pages from Hopi History. Tucson: University of Arizona Press.

Judd, Neil M. 1951. "Nampeyo, An Additional Note." Plateau 24(2):92–93.

——— 1967. The Bureau of American Ethnology, A Partial History. Norman: University of Oklahoma Press.

Laird, W. David, 1977. Hopi Bibliography. Tucson: University of Arizona Press.

"Land Show Is On; Wilson Opens It To All Chicago." Chicago Sunday Tribune. November 20, 1910, 1.

Little, James. 1881. Jacob Hamblin, A Narrative of His Personal Experience as a Frontiersman, Missionary to the Indians, and Explorer. Reprint, 1971. Freeport, N.Y.: Books for Libraries Press.

Lummis, Charles F. 1903. Bullying the Moqui, eds. Robert Easton and Mackenzie Brown, 1968. Prescott, Ariz.: Prescott College Press.

McCluskey, Stephen C. 1980. "Evangelists, Educators, Ethnographers, and the Establishment of the Hopi Reservation." Journal of Arizona

History 21(4):363–90.

McLuhan, T.C. 1985. *Dream Tracks: The Railroad and the American Indian 1890–1930*. New York: Harry N. Abrams.

McNitt, Frank. 1957, 1966. *Richard Wetherill: Anasazi*. Rev. ed. Albuquerque: University of New Mexico Press.

———— 1962. *The Indian Traders*. Norman: University of Oklahoma Press.

Mahood, Ruth I., ed. 1961. *Photographer of the Southwest, Adam Clark Vroman 1856–1916*. New York: Bonanza Books.

Marshall, James. 1945. *Santa Fe, The Railroad that Built an Empire*. New York: Random House.

Means, Florence Crannell. 1960. *Sunlight on the Hopi Mesas*. Philadelphia: Judson Press.

Miller, Helen Markley. 1966. *Lens on the West*. Garden City, N.Y.: Doubleday.

Mindeleff, Cosmos. 1900. "Localization of Tusayan Clans." In *Bureau of American Ethnology 19th Annual Report 1897–98*, 635–53. Washington, D.C.

Mindeleff, Victor. 1891. "A Study of Pueblo Architecture, Tusayan and Cibola." In *Bureau of Ethnology 8th Annual Report 1886–87*, 3–228. Washington, D.C.

Monsen, Frederick. *Frederick Monsen at Hopi*. Reprint #2, 1979. Museum of New Mexico. Reproduced from *The Craftsman* magazine.

Nequatewa, Edmund. 1938. "Dr. Fewkes and Masauwu, the Birth of a Legend." *Museum Notes, Museum of Northern Arizona* 11(2): 25–27.

———— 1943. "Nampeyo, Famous Hopi Potter." *Plateau* 15(3):40–42.

———— "Nampeyo." Manuscript. Colton Collection.

Nichols, Mrs. Frances S., comp. N.p., n.d. *Biography and Bibliography of Jesse Walter Fewkes*.

Oman, Richard G. 1982. "LDS Southwest Indian Art." *Ensign* 2(9):33–37.

Parezo, Nancy J. 1987. "The Formation of Ethnographic Collections: The Smithsonian Institution in the American Southwest." In *Advances in Archaeological Method and Theory*. Vol. 10. San Diego: Academic Press.

Parsons, Elsie Clews. 1921. "Hopi Mothers and Children." *Man* 21(7):98–104.

Patterson, Alex. 1994. *Hopi Pottery Symbols*. Boulder: Johnson Books.

Poling-Kempes, Lesley. 1989. *The Harvey Girls: Women Who Opened the West*. New York: Paragon House.

Powell, John Wesley. 1875. "The Hopi Villages: The Ancient Province of Tusayan." *Scribner's Monthly* 11(2):193–213. Reprint, 1972. Palmer Lake, Colo.: Filter Press.

Schmedding, Joseph. 1951. *Cowboy and Indian Trader*. Caldwell, Idaho: Caxton Printers. Reprint, 1974. Albuquerque: University of New Mexico Press.

Schwartz, Stephen H. 1969. "Nampeo and the Origins of Modern Hopi Pottery." *Lore* 19(4):116–21.

Seaman, P. David, ed. 1993. *Born A Chief*. Tucson: University of Arizona Press.

Smith, Watson. 1971. *Painted Ceramics of the Western Mound at Awatovi*. Papers of the Peabody Museum of Archaeology and Ethnology. Vol. 38. Cambridge: Harvard University.

Smith, Mrs. White Mountain. 1938. "Tom Pavatea, Hopi Trader." *Desert Magazine* 1(4):4–6.

———— 1940. "He Is Our Friend." *Desert Magazine* 4(1):7–10.

Smithsonian Institution. "Annual Report of the Director." *Bureau of Ethnology Annual Report*. Vols. 1–8, 1879–87.

Stanislawski, Michael B., 1979. "Hopi-Tewa." In *Handbook of North American Indians*. Southwest, Vol. 9, 587–602. Washington, D.C.: Smithsonian Institution.

Stanislawski, Michael B., Ann Hitchcock, and Barbara B. Stanislawski. 1976. "Identification Marks on Hopi and Hopi-Tewa Pottery." *Plateau* 48(3–4):47–65.

Stegner, Wallace. 1953, 1954. *Beyond the Hundredth Meridian: John Wesley Powell and the Second Opening of the West*. Boston: Houghton Mifflin.

Stephen, Alexander M. 1936. *Hopi Journal of Alexander M. Stephen*. Ed. Elsie Clews Parsons. New York: Columbia University Press. Reprint, 1969. New York: AMS Press.

Stevenson, James, comp. *Newspaper Clippings, Archaeology of the Southwest*. Scrapbook a. Laboratory of Anthropology Library, Museum of New Mexico, Santa Fe.

———— 1883. "Illustrated Catalogue of the Collection Obtained from the Indians of New Mexico and Arizona in 1879." In *Bureau of Ethnology 2nd Annual Report 1880–81*, 307–

422. Washington, D.C.

Thomas, D. H. 1978. *The Southwestern Indian Detours*. Phoenix: Hunter Publishing.

U.S. Bureau of the Census. *Eleventh Census of the United States, Extra Census Bulletin: Moqui Pueblo Indians of Arizona and Pueblo Indians of New Mexico.* 1893. Washington, D.C.: U.S. Census Printing Office.

U.S. Congress. Senate. *Indian Affairs. Laws and Treaties. Vol. 1 (Laws).* 58th Cong., 2d sess. 1904. Doc. 319.

U.S Department of the Interior. *Commissioner of Indian Affairs to the Secretary of the Interior.* Annual Reports for 1870–74, 1878, 1880–82, 1885, 1887–88, 1890–91, 1894, 1901–6.

——— Correspondence from Superintendent of Moqui Training School and Moqui Agency, 1899 to 1911. Vols. 19–35. Hopi Agency, Keams Canyon.

Wade, Edwin L. 1980. "The Thomas Keam Collection." *American Indian Art* 5(3): 54–61.

——— 1985. "The Ethnic Art Market in the American Southwest 1880–1980." *History of Anthropology: Objects and Others.* Madison: University of Wisconsin Press.

Wade, Edwin L., and Lea S. McChesney. 1980. *America's Great Lost Expedition: The Thomas Keam Collection of Hopi Pottery from the Second Hemenway Expedition 1890–1894.* Phoenix: Heard Museum.

——— 1981. *Historic Hopi Ceramics, The Thomas V. Keam Collection of the Peabody Museum of Archaeology and Ethnology, Harvard University.* Cambridge: Peabody Museum Press.

Walker, Willard, and Lydia I. Wyckoff, eds. 1983. *Hopis, Tewas, and the American Road.* Middletown, Conn.: Wesleyan University.

Waters, Frank. 1963. *Book of the Hopi.* New York: Viking Press. Paperback ed., 1970. New York: Ballantine Books.

Webb, William, and Robert A. Weinstein. 1973. *Dwellers at the Source, Southwestern Indian Photographs of A.C. Vroman 1895–1904.* New York: Grossman Publishers.

Weigle, Marta. 1989. "From Desert to Disney World: The Santa Fe Railway and the Fred Harvey Company Display the Indian Southwest." *Journal of Anthropological Research* 45(1):115–37.

Wright, Barton. 1979. *Hopi Material Culture. Artifacts Gathered by H.R. Voth in the Fred Harvey Collection.* Flagstaff, Ariz.: Northland Press and Heard Museum.

Yava, Albert. 1978. *Big Falling Snow.* Ed. Harold Courlander. Albuquerque: University of New Mexico Press.

The Year of the Hopi, Paintings and Photographs by Joseph Mora 1904–1906. Essays by Frederick Dockstader, Tyrone Stewart, and Barton Wright. 1982. New York: Rizzoli.

Yount, George C. 1923. "The Chronicles of George C. Yount." *California Historical Society Quarterly* 2:3–66. Reprint, 1942. "A Sketch of the Hopi in 1828." *Masterkey* 16(6):193–99.

Index